JOURNAL OF THE
SOUTHWEST

Volume 31, Number 1
Spring 1989

❖

Edited by
Joseph Carleton Wilder

UNIVERSITY OF ARIZONA PRESS
THE SOUTHWEST CENTER
TUCSON

Contents

VOLUME 31, NUMBER 1, SPRING 1989

ENDURING SEEDS

Native American Agriculture and Wild Plant Conservation

By GARY PAUL NABHAN

With a Foreword by WENDELL BERRY

"Gary Nabhan, ethnobotanist, storyteller, cultural historian, Johnny Appleseed, is a seer and celebrant of the cultivated plant world before its defilement by modern agriculture. His interests and insights are as diverse as the wild seeds he gathers. Not only does he write beautifully about what he knows, he also goes out into the fields of native peoples collecting and conserving indigenous seeds, returning them to communities from which they have been lost. In words and actions, Gary Nabhan aims to preserve no less than 'the remaining riches of the living world' and in so doing is a candidate for sainthood." *Gretel Ehrlich*

© Cynthia Farah

Gary Paul Nabhan is the Assistant Director of the Desert Botanical Garden in Phoenix, Arizona, and a cofounder of Native Seeds/SEARCH. He won the John Burroughs Medal for natural history in 1985 for *Gathering the Desert*.

Cloth, $17.95

ALSO AVAILABLE:
The Desert Smells Like Rain
Paper, $8.95

NORTH POINT PRESS, 850 Talbot Avenue, Berkeley, CA 94708

Chinese Sojourners in Territorial Prescott

FLORENCE C. LISTER *and* ROBERT H. LISTER

As the anguish of the American Civil War faded into Reconstruction, there were only three towns of any size in the Arizona Territory, Tucson being the most important. One of the towns was the new, raw, mountain-girded village of Prescott, founded during the war upon orders from President Lincoln to serve as the seat of regional Union government and at the same time to provide protection and supplies for what it was hoped would become active mining operations in the nearby Bradshaw Mountains.

Shortly after Prescott's formal establishment, a grid-patterned town site was laid out across a narrow, pine-dotted valley to the east of an intermittent creek called Granite because of conspicuous rocky formations. The first sale of town lots occurred in June 1864, and names of purchasers were recorded on a map drawn by surveyor Robert Groom. Exhibiting a Yankee sense of order, a few unembellished frame and log structures and corrals were squarely set upon large lots to replace the original, casually erected miners' camps and makeshift stores. A block at the center of the plat was put aside to accommodate a courthouse befitting the Yavapai County seat and so provide a proper focal point for the settlement. As the town grew, the main places of commerce surrounded this plaza. Better-class homes concentrated on gentle hills to its east, and creek banks and low, irregular terraces leading to mountains to the south were left to those of lesser means. It was a well-planned design imposed upon virgin terrain that gradually assumed a midwestern Victorian flavor.

The human composition of Prescott was unlike that of the rest of the Arizona Territory, in which the Hispanic element was domi-

FLORENCE C. LISTER *and* ROBERT H. LISTER *are retired*
Research Associates of Arizona State Museum, now residing in Mancos,
Colorado. "Chinese Sojourners" is an offshoot of their work on the Chinese
community of early Tucson to be published in the Anthropological Papers
of the University of Arizona *by* University of Arizona Press.

nant. With the exception of a small group of Hispanics from New Mexico, most people who followed United States government officials and soldiers to this particular chunk of the frontier had come from the Mississippi valley or farther east. If not born abroad themselves, many had parental roots stretching across western Europe and Canada. Generally, they were first-generation immigrants, bringing with them an accumulated baggage of racial, social, and religious viewpoints. In the main, that included an uncompromising notion of the superiority of themselves and the cultural background from which they emanated.

It comes as a surprise, therefore, to note that on the Groom map of 1864 there appears the name of one Quon Clong Gin as owner of a lot on the rutty lane running along the east side of the creek and hence called Granite Street.[1] Obviously, one of Prescott's founding fathers was an Asian, a fact perhaps deliberately overlooked ever since. Other than his name, absolutely nothing is known about Quon Clong Gin except that Gin is believed to be a Cantonese name, suggesting a south China affiliation. Who he was, where he came from and why, or what he hoped to do with his property remain a tantalizing mystery. Undoubtedly, he was part of the throng of desperate south Chinese who in the mid-nineteenth century had fled their troubled home in search of an elusive pot of gold. Probably he had worked in California and managed to save a modest sum of money, which he dreamed of enlarging into greater security in the growth of Prescott. His dreams must have soured soon, because he was gone by the time the 1870 census was taken.

However, other Chinese in search of livelihood replaced Quon Clong Gin in a Prescott that still was a tiny, isolated village in the midst of a vast, mountainous battleground of hit-and-run Indian warfare. Those physical conditions, added to the unlikelihood of substantial prolonged economic advancement and a cultural background heavily weighed against ethnic accommodation, eventually forced the Chinese to leave. First, there was a half century of coexistence of Occident and Orient on the western Arizona mountain frontier which fell somewhere between the total rejection and exile the Chinese experienced in some territorial mining camps and the adjustments afforded them in the larger diversified centers of Tucson and Phoenix. Nevertheless, much of the history of the Chinese

1. Archives, Sharlot Hall Museum.

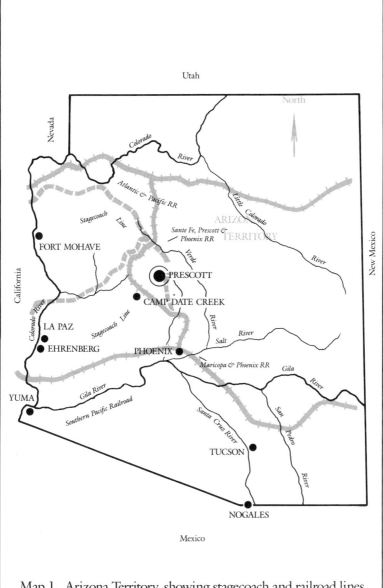

Map 1. Arizona Territory, showing stagecoach and railroad lines connecting with Prescott.

Drawn by Don Bufkin

in Prescott is likewise their history in the larger Arizona Territory.

The initial Chinese arrival in the late 1860s caused a stir among those who likely had never seen a Chinese face to face but who certainly were aware of the animosity swelling against the newcomers in neighboring California. Such an inflow of Chinese, many of their activities over the next half century, and local Euro-American reaction to them were duly recorded by a handful of observant, but often anthropologically ignorant and flagrantly racist, newspapermen. Their journalistic terms for the Chinese—chinks, celestials, johns, Mongolians, or heathens—and creative quotations in pidgin English reflect the pervasive prejudice against these immigrants already felt by the rank-and-file Euro-Americans of the West. Yet a selection of extant press accounts now serves not only as a fulcrum for exploration of the history of this exotic component of borderland society, but also as a basis for examination of certain generalized cultural manifestations peculiar to Chinese civilization. At the same time, the intimacy of small-town reporting affords a unique, highly personal insight into the astounding cultural confrontation of East and West which developed contemporaneously with the opening up of north-central Arizona. Knowledge of individuals who passed through the local Chinese scene is restricted to incomplete scraps of such one-sided newsprint, since the Chinese themselves left no written record, nor has any local deposit of their abandoned material goods been studied.

THE CHINESE ARE HERE

It may be no coincidence that in 1869, when the first contingent of Chinese to follow Quon Clong Gin to Prescott appeared, the Union Pacific Railroad was completed. In that year tracks laid from northern California eastward with the help of Chinese laborers, variously estimated between six and twelve thousand, connected at Promontory in northern Utah with the line punched through from the opposite direction (Figure 1). With this long-distance rail network finally completed, large numbers of Chinese were stranded in the sparsely inhabited interior West with no means of support. Up to this time they had lived in communal work camps along the survey route and had been provided with customary foodstuffs and supplies imported from China by the agents who had contracted for

[Figure 1] A Chinese crew and a Euro-American supervisor are on a Union Pacific Railroad sidecar probably somewhere in north-central Utah. The Orientals have replaced their traditional cotton slippers and loose, thin pants with sturdier boots and heavy trousers needed for the strenuous labors of blasting and grading road-beds through the West's rugged terrain. With this transcontinental railroad completed, some of these laborers may have been among the first Chinese to arrive in Prescott in 1869. *Courtesy* Sharlot Hall Museum.

their services.[2] But on May 10, 1869, their job finished, they were dismissed disinterestedly to fend for themselves as best they could. Most returned to the Pacific coast. A few others traveled eastward on the new rails, eventually to congregate in urban ghettos. Still others gradually dispersed in small groups throughout the spacious intermountain region and moved along with the growing mining frontier.[3] Of these, the greatest number settled temporarily in Idaho, where by 1870 they comprised a third of the population.

2. Kraus 1969: 41–57.
3. Rohe 1982: 5.

Some made their way to Wyoming, to Colorado, or to other places in Utah. News of mineral strikes traveled with mysterious but lightning speed through the camps of the West, so it is surmised that those who showed up in Prescott were part of this body of anchorless men.

If so, they could have made their way south through the sagebrush flats of central Utah and southern Nevada to Hardyville or Fort Mohave, where it was possible to cross the formidable barrier of the Colorado River, in 1869 just being explored further upriver by John Wesley Powell. From these minuscule clusters of buildings at the northern limit of river navigation from the Gulf of California, a toll road cut overland in a southeasterly direction to Prescott (Map 1). Stages and freight wagons were available to bring the Chinese men to town.[4]

In the same period other Chinese were moving along the western border of the Arizona Territory. They may have prompted fellow villagers or relatives to follow them. The 1870 federal census tabulated one Chinese at La Paz and seven at Arizona City (changed to Yuma in 1873) on the Colorado River. Two of them worked on river steamers. One had opened a hotel. Another five Chinese men resided in Vulture City, with one at the Vulture Mine, both located south of Prescott on the desert near modern Wickenburg. One Chinese was recorded in a sweeping southwestern sector of Yavapai County which included Date Creek, Kirkland Valley, and Skull Valley.[5] All these Chinese then in southern Arizona are believed to have moved by steamer across the Gulf of California or to have crossed the Colorado Desert on muleback from the California jumping-off place of San Bernardino. That land route would have brought them to the supply depot of Ehrenburg on the river, where a semiweekly stage made its way 213 miles up through the tiers of rocky arid mountains to Camp Date Creek and then on to evergreen Prescott.[6]

However they came, the local press for the first time confirmed that Chinese were present in the community. Moreover, if one can assume that the reporter reflected popular opinion, it is obvious that negative attitudes toward the Chinese already existed.

4. Walker and Bufkin 1979: 41.
5. U.S. Federal Census, Arizona Territory, 1870.
6. Walker and Bufkin 1979: 41.

We have heretofore neglected to inform our readers that a veritable young Celestial arrived at Fort Whipple a short time ago. Should he live long enough to become a man, Yavapai county will contain one Chinaman.

A real live Chinaman, with tail and other appendages. . . . For our part, we have seen as many of them as we care to see.

Three more Chinamen arrived here during the week, and have gone to work. There are now four of them in this vicinity, which is quite enough.

Since our last, some ten or twelve more Chinamen have arrived.[7]

The report of a lone Chinese youth at Fort Whipple, a post adjacent to Prescott and one of a line of small, insufficiently staffed military installations across territorial Arizona whose purpose was to keep the warlike Indians in check, points to an underlying tragedy behind the overseas movement of the Chinese. Many of those who made the hellish journey in dank vessel holds from China to America were mere children. A comparison of census data giving current age with stated years of residence in the United States shows that it was not uncommon for boys of eight to twelve years of age to have left home and family in the urgent need to earn money abroad. It was the lot of Chinese peasant boys to take a full role in providing for the common good as soon as they were physically capable, but overseas residency meant the added burden of insecurity and loneliness. Many such youngsters never lived to make it back to their homeland. For others, the return trip was delayed for years. For all, it was a too-rapid transition from childhood to manhood.

It was the 1863 discovery of gold which had lured Euro-Americans into this Arizona region, until then an unexplored wilderness. With their previous experience among the mines of California, it was predictable that some of the newly arrived Chinese would hope to share in Prescott's mineral riches. In the condescending prose of the time, a local paper told its readers of one such effort being made in a mining district to the east of town.

---

7. *Arizona Weekly Miner*, May 29, November 27, December 4, 1869; Yoder 1951: 38.

The flight of ye Chinamen is Big Bugwards. John thinks he has struck a big thing there, and is bound to go. Two, three, and four cents to the pan were found by one of them, recently. The finder sent word to his fellow countrymen in Prescott, who, upon learning the glad tidings, held a meeting, discussed the "slubject" and resolved to start immediately, if not sooner. They waited upon their employers and each one said: "Me no likee cookee; no likee washee, any more. Me go Big Bug light away, where one Chinaman telle me he find gleat deal coarse gold. Sabe John. You pay me; me go." They were paid, and went, on their way rejoicing, leaving their employers in the lurch. Now, John, as you have gone out into the woods, we tell you to beware of the Apache.[8]

Placer mining was attractive to the Chinese sojourners because little capital was required beyond the purchase price of shovel, rocker, and pan. Placering already had proved profitable in Prescott's satellite districts, such as Big Bug, Lynx Creek, and the Hassayampa drainage, although the diggings left for the Chinese were worked-over and abandoned or those regarded as sterile. From this disadvantageous practice came the phrase "Chinaman's chance," meaning little chance at all. Ignoring the white miners' snickers, a handful of Chinese workers nevertheless gained a meager livelihood at local placering until the resources were exhausted. With no hint of rancor, the press graciously noted this modest success.

Eight or ten Chinamen are working some placers in the vicinity of the old Ramos farm on Lynx Creek and are doing well.[9]

The farm of pioneers Cornelio and Mary Ramos had been purchased in the 1870s by Chinese Sam Lee and several partners for the sum of three hundred dollars in gold.[10] That considerable investment suggests combined savings accrued over a period of time, perhaps from sustained employment such as railroad construction. When the riffles on Lynx Creek were cleaned out or the seasonal stream went dry, the enterprising Lee and his associate, Ah Fork,

8. *Arizona Weekly Miner*, January 15, 1870.

9. *Arizona Journal Miner*, February 9, 1877.

10. Ramos, of Mexican ancestry, had become a naturalized citizen on October 14, 1868. Index to Minute Record of Orders of Naturalization, 1865 to September 13, 1906, Yavapai County Court House. Potter 1964: 59.

[Figure 2] In 1877 Sam Lee was killed by his partner, Ah Fork, at their saloon on lower Lynx Creek, near where they had panned for gold. Formerly the building had been owned by pioneer settler Mary Ramos, known locally as Virgin Mary. *Courtesy* Sharlot Hall Museum.

opened a one-room saloon and stage station (Figure 2). While living there, Lee is credited with having provided materials to repair wagons of a Euro-American party which had been wrecked during an Apache attack.[11]

Such encounters with Indians were part of daily life on this frontier. Unknowingly, Prescott had been placed in the heart of the traditional lands of the Yavapai, a seminomadic people who expectedly resented Euro-American intrusion and took advantage of every opportunity to eliminate it. Constantly seeking some weakness in Euro-American defenses, the Yavapai hoped to unnerve, if not kill, the settlers, and the Indians' owl hoots and coyote howls could be heard nightly as they communicated with each other from lookouts in the valley around the town. Whenever troops rode out of the tiny Whipple Barracks, Yavapai smoke signals curled along the horizon.[12] To the west of the Yavapai were river tribes, notably the Yuma and Mohave, who made travel through their domain precarious. Several of their massacres of wagon trains received extensive pub-

11. *Arizona Journal Miner*, December 29, 1876.
12. Yoder 1951: 27.

licity. Even more fearsome was the band of western Apache sweeping through the craggy rim country of central Arizona. Throughout the late 1860s and early 1870s they indiscriminately picked off isolated individuals and subjected them to horrible mutilations and deaths.[13] Ranchers, miners, stagecoach passengers, and military scouts were their fair game. The Chinese, too, became victims of these ruthless warriors, who did not recognize the Asians as racial brothers. It is said that the long queues of Chinese black hair merely enhanced the taking of scalps.[14]

The limited number of soldiers skilled in Indian warfare, the rough terrain, and the cleverness of the Native Americans allowed a state of war to continue for years. Not until 1873, when Lieutenant Colonel George Crook and his Whipple Barracks stalwarts finally brought the western bands to reservation life, was there temporary respite from these depredations in the Prescott region. However, within a few years in other districts of the Arizona Territory, the culpability of government Indian agents and contractors wiped out this brief peace. A band of Chiricahua Apaches bolted in rebellion against abuse, fled to the Mexican mountains, and opened a new chapter of conflict that was not ended until 1886. At that time the ringleader, Geronimo, and his men finally surrendered. Prescott was not affected in the second phase of the Apache campaigns except that, until he was replaced, Crook again operated out of Whipple Barracks.

Danger on the frontier notwithstanding, the 1870s saw an increasing influx of Chinese straggling into the remoteness of central Arizona, perhaps drawn there by relayed messages of little open hostility toward others of their race. With an apparent feeling of helplessness and alarm, Euro-American newspapermen kept their readers aware of the oncoming Asian tide. The Prescott *Enterprise* carried such items on September 15 and October 10, 1877.

> Nearly all the stages which have arrived here recently have brought Chinamen as passengers. We hope we are not to be victims of this barbarous horde. We don't admire the Chinese, anyway.
>
> Still they come! Two more Celestials arrived in Prescott on the stage last Sunday morning. The Chinese population of

13. Walker and Bufkin 1979: 38.
14. Fong 1980: 7; 1984: 198–99.

Prescott is getting to be pretty numerous, and unless something is done to stop this immigration they soon will overrun everything.

The rival *Arizona Weekly Miner* noted, on October 26, 1877,

A wagon load of Chinese arrived, today, from the Colorado River, and took up their residences at Mongolian Headquarters on Granite Street. Prescott has over fifty of these pig-tail celestials who live on rice and opium.

Two years later we read,

Prescott has about 75 or 80 Chinamen, which is 75 or 80 too many. Now is a good time to get rid of them.[15]

And the following year:

The coach was loaded down this morning with one Chinaman and emptiness—agreeable companions.[16]

Part of the 1870s surge of Chinese immigrants to the Prescott region was due to construction of the Southern Pacific Railroad, which was planned to run along the thirty-second parallel from Los Angeles to New Orleans. By mid-1877 the tracks had reached the west bank of the Colorado River at Yuma. During a year-long delay while a bridge was being put across the river and permission was being sought to traverse the military reservation on the east side, some of the large Asian labor force deserted camp. Prescott, several hundred miles to the northeast, presented the opportunity for less physically demanding jobs out of the desert heat.

Typically, the Chinese in the American West lived, worked, and relaxed together. That communal settlement pattern often was necessary because of the lack of available or affordable housing in communities just being carved out of the frontier. The Chinese were probably not disturbed by such an arrangement, because men's and boys' houses were commonplace in the south China region from which they had come.[17] Perhaps more important in the West, such houses served as a defense against an unfamiliar and often unfriendly outside world. All these factors may have been at work in

15. *Arizona Weekly Miner*, October 3, 1879.
16. *Arizona Weekly Miner*, July 16, 1880.
17. Prazniak 1984: 124.

Prescott, where in 1870 there were just 151 widely dispersed dwellings. One might have been on the lot on the east side of Granite Street between Gurley and Goodwin streets which had been purchased by Quon Clong Gin. Several ramshackle buildings across Granite Street were available for rent, one formerly a butcher shop operated by Euro-American pioneer Guilford Hathaway. Thus when other Chinese began drifting into town, this is the district to which they were attracted and where they were to remain concentrated during their entire stay. Although no residential restrictions were placed on the new Asian migrants, it conveniently happened that the area they favored already was considered by Euro-Americans to be a less desirable part of town, even though it was just one block from the plaza, and the seat of territorial government at times would be immediately across the stream to the west of Granite Street. A map of 1890 confirms earlier references to the block on Granite Street between Gurley and Goodwin streets as Prescott's small Chinatown (Map 2).

The Chinese occupied a half dozen frame buildings on the west side of Granite Street. In each case a small room opening onto the dirt street in front served as a place of business. In the rear, a variable number of men lived in one or more rooms modified with wooden bunks along the walls and pegs upon which clothes could be hung. A wood stove provided heat, essential in the brief winters typical of the five-thousand-foot elevation. A simple, common kitchen contained cooking stove, table, chairs, storage shelves, and utensils. Probably there was some sort of a small altar in the bedroom and an image of the kitchen god in the cooking area to whom cursory recognition was offered. A few family pictures, cheap prints torn from Chinese-language publications, or lunar calendars adorned walls. Otherwise, the cellular rooms were devoid of ornamentation but were cluttered from overcrowding and infrequent housecleaning. Privies stood out back along the creek. Kitchen gardens, stray chickens, and stables shared the yards. In general, these meager quarters were no better, and certainly no worse, than those the Chinese knew in their homeland. Nor were they appreciably inferior to others occupied by much of the Euro-American bachelor population.

At some undetermined period the building on the second lot on Granite Street north from Goodwin acquired the distinction of a second story fronted by a porch. An elevated false roofline across

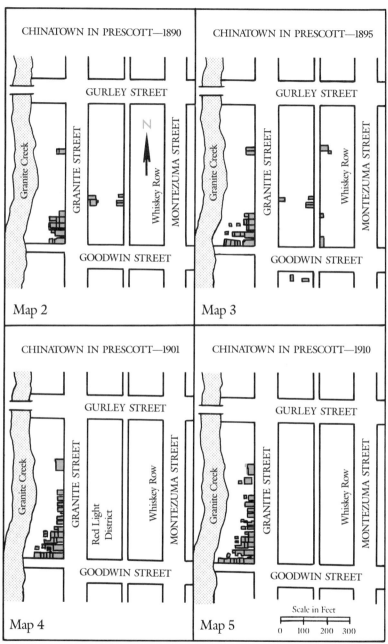

CHINATOWN IN PRESCOTT—1890

GURLEY STREET

Granite Creek

GRANITE STREET

N

Whiskey Row

MONTEZUMA STREET

GOODWIN STREET

Map 2

CHINATOWN IN PRESCOTT—1895

GURLEY STREET

Granite Creek

GRANITE STREET

Whiskey Row

MONTEZUMA STREET

GOODWIN STREET

Map 3

CHINATOWN IN PRESCOTT—1901

GURLEY STREET

Granite Creek

GRANITE STREET

Red Light District

Whiskey Row

MONTEZUMA STREET

GOODWIN STREET

Map 4

CHINATOWN IN PRESCOTT—1910

GURLEY STREET

Granite Creek

GRANITE STREET

Whiskey Row

MONTEZUMA STREET

GOODWIN STREET

Scale in Feet

0   100   200   300

Map 5

Based upon Sanborn Fire Insurance Maps, Sanborn–Perris Map Co., New York

the facade bearing simple scrolled decoration was the only modifica-
tion hinting at anything other than the usual building to be found
in any western frontier town (Figures 3, 4). Presumably, this upper
level and its elaboration were ordered and paid for by Chinese
tenants to serve as their meeting hall, where both religious and
social activities could take place. Such installations were common in
their native villages of south China. They assumed even greater
importance in the American West as group rallying places.

Inside the rooms, considered by Euro-Americans to be a temple,
was undoubtedly a clay or wooden image of the god Kuan Yu (also
Kuan Ti or Kuan Kung), one of a hierarchy of idols termed *josses*.
Kuan Yu was a legendary military hero of the Three Kingdoms
believed to exemplify masculinity. Usually he was portrayed as a
red-faced, bewhiskered individual in a seated position. Kuan Yu
likely was accompanied by one or more altars and votive tables,
banners with inscriptions, lanterns, long sandalwood tapers (or joss
sticks) stuck into brass urns of sand to be slivered as incense, red
candles, perhaps a barrel-shaped umbrella (a symbol of respect or
purity), red paper prayer slips and a furnace for their burning, and a
gong and drum on a wooden stand.[18] The most educated man of
the group probably was the guardian of the so-called temple, with
responsibilities for burning incense, lighting candles, pouring rice
wine, and interpreting divination signs for determining propitious
dates for burial of the dead or for proposed activities.

Opposite this complex of structures, on the east side of Granite
Street, was a boardinghouse indicated by Sanborn fire-insurance
mappers as Chinese, and at least three additional Chinese-occupied
dwellings faced the alley behind. They are believed to have been on
what was once the Quon Clong Gin land. By 1890, scattered to the
north and south of this core of Chinatown were ten other buildings
used by the Asians as joint work and sleeping space. Their locations
may have been determined by those of the clients served. Other
Chinese were provided spartan housing at their places of employment. Everywhere, whether on Granite Street or more removed, it
was mere subsistence-level survival, uncomfortable as it was un-
healthful. But as the Chinese wanted, or perhaps as social and
economic conditions mandated, it was together.

The Chinese who settled in Prescott were quick to see that the

18. Culin 1890a: 40–41; Lee 1960; Wells 1971.

[Figure 3] The heart of Prescott's Chinatown in the late 1870s or early 1880s was a row of four buildings: two gable-roofed with typical Western-style false fronts and two flat-roofed brick, along the west side of a rocky Granite Street. The central two-story building served as the local temple, or joss house. Scrollwork was added to the top of the facade, over which was raised a flagpole bearing the banner of the local tong. A group of three boys stands before the left building, while a fourth walks on stilts in front of the joss house. The man in the shadows probably was a Chinese tenant residing behind one of the businesses along this street. *Courtesy* Sharlot Hall Museum.

resident Euro-American population, in a ratio of five males to one female, routinely got hungry and dirty but had no inclination to tend to these needs. Recognizing that cooking and washing required little specialized skill and only a minimal command of English, these migrants, like other Chinese throughout the mountain West, formed small-scale food and laundry service industries that were to flourish for the entire lifetime of the local Chinese community. As the enterprises expanded, they included related activities ranging from dishwashing to raising vegetables, from ironing to delivering cleaned garments. The 1870 federal census revealed that, out of a total Prescott population of 668 persons, there were six Chinese already engaged in these tasks. A. He Sing, Ali Tung,

[Figure 4] By the late 1880s a third brick building had been added on the north end of the Chinatown row, and the joss house flagpole had been replaced by a very tall free-standing pole in the street in front. The building on the south had been refurbished with new siding and a sign reading "Chinese Store." Within a little more than a decade, the principal activities of gambling and smoking opium were taking place behind the token grocery store in the front room. The horse-drawn wagon hitched to a post was the type used by farmers from the Miller Valley Chinese Gardens to peddle their fresh produce to the town's private homes and restaurants. *Courtesy* Sharlot Hall Museum.

and Wo Sam said they were cooks. Whether they had found work in kitchens of boardinghouses, restaurants, or private homes is not known. Ah Lee, Ah Poy, and Ah Hin were laundrymen, who may have plied their trade in private homes. The average age of these immigrants was between twenty-nine and thirty years. All had been born in China. Because clan or village members customarily colonized together, it is assumed they had been personally acquainted before they reached Arizona. It is also assumed that they were speakers of the Sze Yap dialect, inasmuch as those persons were most numerous among the incoming lower-class migrants. The devastating Taiping Rebellion centered in south China had driven them out of their homeland.

Even though terrorized by Indians and suffering prolonged effects of national economic depression, in the 1870s Prescott was a lively place where day or night at any number of bars a thirsty man could get a shot of liquor. The block along the west side of the plaza on Montezuma Street was becoming a wooden wall of rowdy drinking, gambling, and cavorting establishments known to one and all as Whiskey Row and peopled with the cast of mismatched characters that made the Old West the stuff of drama. Many saloonkeepers added eateries in the knowledge that even cowboys in town for relaxation, off-duty soldiers, or miners celebrating a find could not live by drink alone. The eager Chinese were in luck, being in the right place at the right time. In short order, they took over management or operation of these saloon restaurants, either employed by Euro-American owners or leasing their facilities. A talent for pleasing American palates cheaply added the phrases "chop house" and "noodle joint" to the upland vocabulary.

Daily, another growing corps of Chinese laundrymen worked in shabby, frame washhouses, their yards filled with drying platforms and pools of sudsy water. The more aggressive of the washermen displayed a characteristic Chinese taste for partnerships, with three or four men forming a joint business venture.[19] Combined resources provided the necessary funds for supplies of soap, firewood, and a few pieces of equipment. Partners were apt to have been related by clan or village. Proprietorship gave them the satisfaction of self-employment, a desirable status enhancement for those who formerly may have known only peasant background. It also allowed the option of the requisite trip back to China for family visits, while the endeavor continued to function in the hands of the others. These instances of group effort usually involved a division of labor in which some men washed, some ironed, and an apprentice, generally newly arrived in America, learned how to do both satisfactorily.

One solo laundry owner was Ah Sam, who had the foresight to set up shop next to the town jail. An entry in the Proceedings of the Board of Supervisors shows his receipt of $16.45 for washing done for prisoners confined there.[20]

As Paul Siu points out,[21] each laundry was a microcosm of China. Men tied by blood or territorial relationships worked side by side all day, ate and slept side by side at night, were concerned for each other's welfare, and together recalled home and times past.

19. Light 1972: 93.
20. *Arizona Weekly Miner*, October 7, 1871.
21. Siu 1952: 34–44; 1964: 429–42.

Except for sporadic encounters with Euro-American customers, they were out of touch with the culture around them. In the absence of their own firsthand impressions, their personal reactions to that situation remain unknown. If they fit the sojourner profile described by Siu, they considered themselves outsiders, and the Euro-Americans thought of them only in relation to their jobs and not to their individual personages.

George Ah Fat was one of the few early immigrants to Prescott who can be viewed as an up-and-coming entrepreneur. With several partners, he placed what may have been the first commercial advertisement of a Chinese-owned business in Prescott. He likely had a ghost writer, but there is no doubt that he had learned the value of western-style promotion. The advertisement, which appeared in the September 2, 1871, edition of the *Arizona Weekly Miner*, read,

New Laundry
Granite Street   Prescott, Arizona
George Ahfat & Co.

Wash every class of fabric at their New Laundry Ladies' clothing flooted by flooting machine [*sic?*] in a manner to suit the most fastidious. Shirt bosoms, etc. polished and made to show well. Terms reasonable. Public patronage solicited.

The Ah Fat enterprise must have prospered, because on February 16, 1877, the same paper told its readers,

> George Ah Fat gave a new year's dinner today, at which, he informed us yesterday, he intended among other delicacies to serve tea that costs $10 per pound.

Success, however, had its price. For unknown reasons, the industrious Ah Fat had acquired an enemy. The *Enterprise* of March 21, 1877, carried this brief item.

> An attempt was made last Saturday to blow up the wash-house belonging to George Ah Fat. It is supposed to have been made by another Chinaman. There was no harm done, beyond the charring of some timbers.

Then reenter Sam Lee, as a follow-up article revealed.

> Sam Lee, the Lynx Creek Chinaman, who was arrested on a complaint made by George Ah Fat, to the effect that said Lee tried to blow up said Ah Fat's house, with a can of powder,

has been held to answer to the charge before the next Grand Jury. Bail was set at $1,000 and not being able to produce the necessary bonds he was remanded to jail.[22]

That matter apparently resolved, at summer's end Sam Lee's troubles were to come to a violent conclusion.

On Sunday afternoon an altercation took place between two almond-eyed sons of the Flowery Land, named, respectively Sam Lee and Ah Fork. The disturbance was about ownership of some property, and as usual, there was a woman mixed up in the affair. Sam Lee commenced the trouble and struck Ah Fork three times with a knife, severely wounding him. Ah Fork, having procured a knife, struck Sam Lee with it, killing him instantly. Coroner Day, with a jury, held that the homicide was justifiable.[23]

The bits of information available strongly suggest that the two men shared the attentions of one of the rare Chinese women in the northern territory. Anxieties over pleasures, rather than business, may have led to the fracas. To continue the Sam Lee saga,

Ah Fork, who it will be remembered killed Sam Lee, his brother Celestial, at Lynx Creek recently, has been re-arrested and is now in jail. Ah Fork was allowed to go free upon the verdict of the coroner's jury, but subsequent investigation has revealed the fact that his release was the result of crooked swearing or interpretation. The Grand Jury, on reassembling, will have a chance at him.

The case of Ah Fork for the murder of Sam Lee was examined on Tuesday by Justice Cate. The prisoner was discharged, there being no evidence to convict him of the offense. The prosecuting witness, Ah Key, testified that the reason he had sworn out a warrant charging Ah Fork with murder was that he had a dispute with him about a wagon.

The property of Sam Lee, recently killed on Lynx Creek, will be sold tomorrow evening by C. F. Cate, public admin-

22. *Enterprise*, March 21, 1877.
23. *Enterprise*, August 22, 1877.

istrator. There is a good span of horses and wagon in the outfit.[24]

Two years later a touching postscript to the sad Lee affair was reported by the local paper.

> R. J. Rutherford, the pioneer expressman, this morning per-formed the pious duty of taking two of the followers of Con-fucius, with a lot of roast pig, peaches, grapes and a bottle of brandy to Lynx Creek to feed a dead countryman, who has lain beneath the cold gravel of that lonely canyon, where he was murdered, a whole year [*sic*], without a morsel of food or a drop of anything to cheer him on his journey to that flowery kingdom where all good Chinamen at last bring up.
> Rutherford says there was no thrown off about the feed: they left plenty of it, and that which was good, on the grave, and as the two live celestials returned to town with him, there is no probability of their returning to bring away what their defunct friend may have left after satisfying his appetite.[25]

Placing food in or on the graves of the dead for the soul's journey to the nether world was a customary practice in China going back at least as far as the Bronze Age.[26] Uninformed Euro-American associ-ates of the Chinese were merely bemused that costly edibles could be squandered by men having little money. They did not realize it was one more expression of the unquestioning adherence on the part of the Chinese to their Confucian moral obligations to friends and family. The men who went out to the Lynx Creek grave may well have shared the Lee surname.

As for George Ah Fat, whose house the deceased allegedly torched, he gave up laundering and went into the restaurant busi-ness next to a saloon owned by D. C. Thorne. The 1880 census showed him managing a Montezuma Street eatery and overseeing four Chinese cooks, who probably shared his investment. That change of trade would have been considered by both Euro-Americans and Asians as a step up the social and economic scale. Unfortunately, the following item suggests that abuse by Euro-American customers drove him and his colleagues away and that the

24. *Enterprise*, August 29, September 1, September 5, 1877.
25. *Arizona Weekly Miner*, September 5, 1879.
26. Culin 1890b: 195.

racial prejudice present from the beginning of the Prescott Chinese colony had not been eradicated through greater familiarity.

> George Ah Fat & Co., of the Cabinet Chop House, desire us to state that they have concluded to make an unconditional surrender, and will, after this evening, cease to run the boarding department of the Cabinet.[27]

Cooking was an honorable profession in China requiring long apprenticeship, but most of those who initially took up this occupation in America had no such training. Adaptable and ingenious, they generally were peasants or small tradesmen whose lives on the borderlands of famine had taught them how to make something palatable out of virtually nothing. This experience stood them in good stead in frontier kitchens. In contrast, laundering, as practiced by Chinese in the West, carried with it the stigma of having been nonstop woman's work in the homeland. When men engaged in such work went back to China, they often were scorned.[28] However, on the west coast both these trades became strictly controlled by Chinese guilds regulating apprenticeships, wages, prices, and locations. The first bloody riot within the San Francisco Chinatown was between laundrymen protesting areal restrictions imposed by a guild.[29] Additionally, Chinese district or clan associations had the power to sanction or deny a person's participation in either line of work.[30] Records are lacking to confirm the presence of any similar work structure in Prescott, but it is evident that a labor stratification based upon white racial attitudes was operative, and it essentially denied the Chinese much opportunity to demonstrate their true worth.

Some of the Euro-American attitudes toward the cooking and washing occupations were unyielding. This was tough country, where manliness was equated with wielding a pick or ax, riding herd, fighting Indians, or beating a team of mules into obedience. In the code of time and place, slaving over the proverbial hot stove or scrub board was not manly. Doing these tasks placed the Chinese in the most lowly servile status, even though the services rendered were essential to the daily functioning of the bachelor-dominated,

27. *Arizona Weekly Miner*, July 16, 1880.
28. Lee 1960: 81.
29. Dillon 1962: 100–101.
30. Light 1972: 91–92.

roominghouse culture. "No tickee, no launlee" stereotyped the overseas Chinese to many Americans, even after they had graduated to other work.

It was not merely the means by which these immigrants at the bottom rungs of the ladder were existing and flourishing that fueled anti-Chinese sentiment. One root problem was, on the one hand, a perplexing lack of interest on the part of Asians in what to most red-blooded Euro-American citizens were the obvious benefits of Americanization and Christianity, and, on the other, a staunch belief among Euro-Americans in the necessity of racial, cultural, linguistic, and religious conformity in order for the nation to prosper. These feelings were intensified by many highly visible physical and ethnic distinctions between themselves and the Chinese. The frontier's towering, brawny Swedes, Germans, or Irishmen often interpreted the generally short stature, slight build, straggling whiskers, scurrying gait, and hand gestures of the southern Chinese as signs of weakness. The weak were not countenanced in this environment.

Furthermore, Chinese dialects were harsh to western ears; their several thousand written characters, brushed rather than penned, were incomprehensible. In the early years, many overseas Chinese did not learn English, nor did they have any motivation for doing so inasmuch as they operated within their own sphere. That caused resentment among Euro-Americans, a feeling irrationally heightened by their own lack of understanding of the Chinese language. Most of the immigrants who in the course of a day had to deal with Euro-Americans managed to learn a few key English words or phrases, but their difficulties of pronunciation provided the basis for endless belittling imitations. The biased frontier press, among them the Prescott newspapers, fueled this cruel parody.

Chinese names also were a constant source of confusion for westerners, as well as for those now attempting to reconstruct overseas Chinese history. Not only were they difficult to transcribe into English, but often it was not realized that the Chinese reversed the order so that surnames typically preceded personal names.[31] This was the Chinese way of immediate clan identification. Moreover, for a variety of reasons, the immigrants sometimes chose not to go by the appellations given them in China. As a consequence, many names surviving in records are corruptions, reversals, nicknames,

31. Lee 1960: 135.

anglicizations, and outright falsifications.[32] Strings of aliases litter extant documents. It appears that if a Chinese man was called Charley or Joe by some chance Euro-American acquaintance, he kept that name for the duration of his stay in the United States. Or he simply took the name of some Euro-American of whom he may have heard. How else can one explain the fact that a Cantonese who worked as a cook in La Paz in 1870 was known as Joseph Smith unless he had passed through Zion or met a waggish Mormon en route to the Colorado River? How can one account for a Prescott caterer's being Fong Murphy? It is particularly intriguing that a high percentage of the immigrants told paymasters, census takers, or other Euro-American record keepers that their personal names were Ah. Actually, Ah is not a proper name but a term of endearment or a nickname used by Cantonese. Perhaps simply because it was easy for English speakers to write and spell, the Ahs definitely had it. Half of the Chinese men and one woman tabulated in the 1880 Prescott census went by that name, one even being Ah Ah.

The typical garb of the Chinese laborer and his mandatory queue starkly signaled his uniqueness to the Euro-American frontiersman (Figure 5). Usual clothing consisted of a dark blue, loose cotton tunic (*san*), untailored cotton pants (*koo*), soft dark sandals, white socks, and either a skull cap or a conical rice-straw hat. Added warmth was supplied by a quilted, waist-length, cotton jacket fastened down the front with loops. These clothes were ideal for subtropical southern China, but they did not suit more severe climates or rugged labors in thorny or rocky terrain. Chinese men faced with these conditions in western America gradually acquired mixed assortments of sturdy boots, denim trousers, wool jackets, and broadbrimmed, black felt hats, but traditional Chinese garments were retained for festive occasions.

Because ingrained food habits generally are relinquished only under duress, the local Chinese surely made every effort to eat as they did in Guangdong or Fujian provinces. With trade channels expanding during the territorial period, they were able to secure their preferred supplies from intermediaries on the west coast who depended upon Asian business. Red meat, potatoes, fried eggs, and boiling coffee may have been dished out by Chinese cooks on Whiskey Row, but on Granite Street the diet undoubtedly was rice, soy

32. Lyman 1974: 110.

[Figure 5] This unidentified man was among the Chinese sojourners who came to Prescott in the late 1870s. His dress, typical of nineteenth-century Chinese commoners, consists of an ample, line, high-necked, felt tunic with frog fasteners and inordinately long sleeves; untailored cotton trousers tied around the ankles; flat-soled cotton or felt slippers; white stockings; and skullcap. Wearing this outfit, thousands of his countrymen came to the West in a desperate search for lucrative jobs. This solemn-faced individual holds some undetermined object in his right hand that may have had symbolic significance. The photographer, D. F. Mitchell, supplied what he considered props suitable to his subject: a water pipe and two porcelain, lidded tea cups with overglaze decoration. Quite surely they had been acquired locally from one of the recently opened Chinese stores on Granite Street. *Courtesy* Sharlot Hall Museum.

sauce, peanut oil, bean sprouts, preserved duck eggs, dried sea crea-
tures, barbecued pork, pickled cabbage, and gallons of green tea. As
if that were not affront enough to Euro-American sensitivities,
chopsticks replaced forks, cups had no handles, flat saucepans gave
way to round-bottomed woks, and razor-sharp cleavers sliced
through bone and gristle.

With their often-recounted ethnocentrism, the sojourners in
Prescott, like their countrymen trying to survive in other sectors of
the western frontier, can be interpreted as outwardly indifferent to
what Euro-Americans thought of them and their ways as long as it
did not involve personal harm or forfeiture of dreams. Because most
anticipated being away from their homeland just long enough to
accumulate a stake, they seemed to cultivate a detachment from
American affairs which made Euro-American associates edgy. Luck
and ability both played a part in their monetary success, but in the
meantime, the overseas Chinese demonstrated their intention of
pursuing familiar paths, making accommodations to American life-
styles only as necessary for existence or to accomplish certain ill-
defined economic goals.

For many, those goals became increasingly vague and unachiev-
able through time.[33] Opportunities in a small, out-of-the-way town
like Prescott, without agricultural, fishing, lumbering, or manufacturing potential, always were limited. Added to the narrow economic base was the fact that racial stereotypes already in place
before the Chinese appeared on the local scene restricted them to a
few services. Thus, partly by choice and partly because of racism,
the immigrants were essentially isolated, although at the same time
they were symbiotically dependent on a dominant society that was
itself economically undiversified and struggling to survive. Here
were seeds for future trouble.

Regardless of race, the way of life for many men on the frontier
was stressful. For members of all groups, social control often broke
down into crimes against each other. The Chinese had a further
burden: they had come to America with a deep-rooted habit of
intragroup quarreling. Lineages, villages, secret societies, and individuals typically were enmeshed in feuds and vendettas that had
bloodied generations.[34] That resort to easy violence was transferred

33. Siu 1952: 34–44.
34. Culin 1890b: 193; Kraus 1969: 56–57; Lyman 1974: 15, 50–52.

to the American West, although the immigrants did not wear guns strapped about their hips as did their Euro-American contemporaries. Instead, in fits of rage they had no hesitancy about grabbing any object—ax, pick, or knife—and taking after an enemy. Some proved to be fair shots once guns were acquired. Eventually, the salaried soldiers of the Chinese tongs became the fiercest of all fighting men in the West.[35]

For the Chinese, the difference between home and the Arizona Territory was that disputes in the latter, especially those involving personal attacks, ideally were settled in court. Even though they distrusted courts, lawyers, and officials, the sojourners found the American way beneficial. In China there was no leniency toward commoners who disturbed the public order, only savage physical punishment meted out without due process.[36] In contrast, the bulk of the Chinese in the United States were self-proclaimed transients and without citizenship. Yet they were given the protection of American law. That necessarily also entailed the obligation to observe it, often something of a problem for these aliens, who were prone to resort to extralegal methods against their countrymen.[37]

Prescott's newspapers vacillated between straightforward reporting of such internal Chinatown troubles and patronizing verbiage. In either case, there was a quality of small-town gossip. The following selection indicates the range of conflict but is not intended to imply any greater degree of lawlessness on the part of the Asians than among fellow Euro-Americans, some of whom seemed bent on giving Prescott a reputation for wildness. A relevant statistic is that in 1899 there were 228 prisoners in the territorial prison in Yuma, of whom only two were Chinese.[38] Even in California, where the infamous tong wars raged during the late nineteenth century, relatively few Chinese were incarcerated. The offenses noted by the Prescott press pale by comparison.

Hee King was fined $50 and costs last Saturday in Justice Otis's court, for stealing $25 from another Chinaman.

This week, Justice Fleury has recorded an unusual amount of criminal business. On Wednesday, he completed the examina-

---

35. Dillon 1962: 167.
36. Bluden and Elvin 1983: 148; Clayre 1984: 9.
37. Culin 1890b: 193.
38. *Arizona Republican*, October 24, 1899.

tion of two chinamen, charged with applying a hatchet to the head of another Celestial, and which case had been on the docket for several days. After having listened to the conflicting stories usual in such cases, and finding that he lacked jurisdiction to guillotine the whole outfit, discharged one of the defendants, and suffered the other, together with the complainant, to pay a fine of fifty dollars each, with the alternative of fifty days in the county jail.

Two Celestials with unpronounceable names, last night got into a difficulty in the rear of Tompkin's saloon, which resulted in one of the combatants receiving an ugly wound on the head from a shovel in the hands of his adversary. Arrest was made late last night by Marshal Dodson of the Chinaman who used the shovel and an examination will be held to-day before Justice Fleury.

The Chinaman who committed the assault last night and whose name is Ah Fun, was examined to-day before Judge Fleury, plead guilty to the charge, was fined $100 and not responding with the amount levied will spend the ensuing fifty days in the county jail. He is reported to have recently come here from Los Angeles, is a Chinese desperado of the highbinder type, and the court felt the necessity of making an example of him to deter future lawlessness among his compatriots.

Joe Jung, who committed an assault on Tung Young this morning, was brought before Judge Fleury and fined $50. In default of the necessary funds, wherewith to pay the fine, he was politely escorted to the county jail, with permission to assist in watering the young shade trees around the plaza, for a term of fifty days.[39]

While generally on peaceful but impersonal terms, Prescott's Euro-Americans and Chinese experienced some minor clashes that took on racial overtones. Although the papers tended to side with

39. *Arizona Weekly Miner*, September 3, 1875; March 5, 1880; August 6, 1880. A highbinder was a Chinese urban hired gun in the employment of a group, or tong, engaged in criminal activities. The term may have derived from the custom of binding the queue to the top of a man's head so that it could not be grasped by an assailant. Dicker 1979: 15.

the former, it is to their credit that this was not invariably the case, particularly in instances such as the one recounted below when Asians obviously were victimized.

> Monday night last, at a Chinese wash-house, on Granite Street, three tea and opium inspired devils from the Flowery Land, attacked a countryman of theirs, who had sawed off his tail, cut him up horribly and would have killed him outright had not Jennings, the night watchman, rushed in and stopped the war. The tailless Chinaman's wounds were dressed by Dr. Kendall, who informs us that they were sufficiently numerous and dangerous to have put an end to any man or living thing save a Chinaman. Arrests were made by Jennings, but we believe that all the flesh-chopping scoundrels are now at large.
>
> In connection with this affair, there is considerable talk among citizens, regarding Jennings' action, to get possession of certain cash belonging to one or more of the Chinese—said action, some say, being very similar to that in vogue among burglars and highwaymen.

> Nightwatchman Jennings wishes us to state that in taking money from Chinese depositories, on the night of the fracas, he had acted according to the urgent request of the Chinaman whom the others had tried to kill, and who, by the way, is now at the point of death.

> One of our citizens made several "honest pennies" out of the recent Chinese row, in this way: one "John" wished some arrests made, the citizen in question pretended to be a peace officer, and would not move in the matter until the complaining heathen paid him $10, which he did. Our cute cit. [citizen] then went and button-holed one of the pugnacious "Johns" until said "John" paid him $5, when Mr. Cit. let him go. While this action cannot be claimed as legitimate, it will, perhaps, prove to be good experience to the Celestials.

> Private Peter Ness, of Company C, 23d Infantry, died at Fort Whipple hospital, on the 10th inst., from the effects of a gun-shot wound recently inflicted upon him by a Chinaman, at this place, which Chinaman was, on Thursday last, examined

by Justice Otis and remanded to jail, to await trial for the killing of Ness.

The Chinaman who is accused of killing the late Peter Ness, is now out on bail. His counsel, Capt., J. P. Hargrave, applied to district court commissioner, Ed. W. Wells, for a writ of habeas corpus, on the ground of unlawful imprisonment, when, after examining witnesses and listening to the arguments of Capt. Hargrave, for the writ, and those of Judge Carter against, admitted the prisoner to bail in the sum of $1,500, with J. E. G. Mitchell and Guilford Hathaway as sureties.

This action will save some county expense. There are no fears that the Chinaman will skedaddle, it being pretty generally conceded that it will be hard to convict him of murder.

Kim Wa, a Celestial, and a U.S. soldier had a dispute and skirmish on the street this morning, over a wash bill. The Chinaman got the best of the fray.

Last Monday night three Chinamen attacked the cook of the Fort Whipple band, and were about converting him into a gelatinous mass, when several chivalric Frenchmen, who were standing in front of Eymarie's saloon, came boldly to the rescue, drove the Chinese horde away and rescued the unfortunate from the clutches of the heathen. Vive la France.

Hon. J. H. Behan had occasion to call at the Chinese laundry this P.M., when a controversy arose, leading to some half dozen of the pig-tail race making an assault on him with clubs. He tried to defend himself with a revolver, which unfortunately, failed to work. He received several severe cuts about the head. Four of his assailants were arrested and lodged in jail.

The Chinese washermen, some ten or twelve, who attacked J. H. Behan yesterday were on trial to-day before Justice Cate. After considerable testimony was taken the case went over until to-morrow.[40]

40. *Arizona Weekly Miner*, January 20, 27, 1872; January 25, March 15, March 22, December 19, 1873; August 1, October 3, 1879.

Lonely and far from familiar places and the family that was the hub of their social organization, the Chinese of the West turned to three principal forms of recreation: paid sex, gambling, and smoking opium. Participation in one or all sometimes absorbed the monies being saved for home. Prescott's papers had little to say about the first two activities; they also were standard attributes of Euro-American frontier life.[41]

The Chinese movement to America was primarily one of young men. It has been estimated that in California about half of them were married, but statistics for Prescott reveal that in the initial period of Chinese presence there were more than twice as many single than married sojourners.[42] Wives of the latter had been left in China for economic and social reasons. At the outset, there was not enough money to pay two passages. Few lower-class women wanted to venture beyond the customary security of their husband's extended family circle, and they were unprepared to withstand the physical rigors of frontier life.[43] Whereas almost thirty-five thousand Chinese men had reached the west coast early in the 1860s, only sixteen Chinese women had braved the journey.[44] Lyman states that between 1850 and 1882 one hundred thousand Chinese men were in America, as opposed to 8,848 women.[45] Married men, thus, were faced with an unnatural sexual curtailment. The chances for single sojourners to meet respectable Chinese female companions in the United States were virtually nil. Theoretically, mates for them could not be sought in other races because miscegenation was legally prohibited in thirty states, as well in the Arizona Territory.[46] One consequence of the gender imbalance was prostitution.[47]

At first the Chinese men sought out Euro-American, Negro, and Hispanic women who did not maintain racial barriers among their customers. Then, beginning in middle of the nineteenth century,

41. In 1864, of 36 adult females in the Third Judicial District that encompassed Prescott, 14 were known prostitutes. U.S. Federal Census, Arizona Territory, 1864. Historical Records Survey, Phoenix, 1938.

42. U.S. Federal Census, Arizona Territory. Prescott, 1880: married Chinese males 29, single Chinese males 62; 1900: married Chinese males 111, single Chinese males 121; 1910: married Chinese males 74, single Chinese males 53.

43. Lyman 1970: 18.

44. Lee 1949: 422–32; Wegars 1984.

45. Lyman 1970: 18.

46. Lyman 1974: 91.

47. Wegars 1984.

numerous Chinese women were sold into slavery, kidnapped, or duped into coming illegally into the United States under the auspices of secret societies reaping tremendous financial profits from a fleshpot traffic that was permitted to flourish by corrupt or indifferent American officials. For decades, these so-called singsong girls[48] represented virtually the total immigration of Chinese females. One exception was a limited number of merchant wives, who were kept in tight seclusion because they, too, were preyed upon by slavers.[49]

One protest came from a Prescott reporter.

The importation of Chinese women for immoral purposes is a crying disgrace to the United States and to American civilization. It is a so-called civilized Government acting the part of procuress, but although the better sense of the country has long cried out against it, the infamous traffic still continues.[50]

The scarcity of Chinese women led to other deviant behavior. Cases of polyandry, more than one man to a wife, are known. That may have been the circumstance behind the murder of Sam Lee on Lynx Creek. Probably more common were jealous squabbles of the sort described below in the journalistic sarcasm of the day.

Lots of fun for the whites of Prescott, this week, and heap vexation of spirit for the Chinese portion of our population. The business came up in this way: Several months ago, there dwelt at Los Angeles, California, a rather prepossessing damsel, of small stature, and (county recorder Wells informs us), smaller feet. So-Sing-Sing-Hoy, the feminine in question, was seen and admired by Ah-Own, who, according to his tale (no allusion to his pig-tail) presented himself before her, and, offering her his heart, hand and the largest part of his "licy", had his proposal accepted, took So-Sing-Sing-Hoy home with him and put her in his little bed. Weeks rolled on, as a novel donkey would say, and the happy twain grew unhappy in each other's bosoms. The climate, or something else, was not favorable to the growth of love between them, besides the terrible

---

48. Dillon 1962: 141, 169.
49. Lyman 1974: 89.
50. *Enterprise*, August 26, 1877.

Los Angeles riot, in which so many Chinese were slaughtered, scared these two Celestials out of their sandals, and they turned their faces toward Arizona; arrived, in due time, at Wickenburg, and were there living as harmoniously as two rival Tom Cats, until a Prescott Chinaman named Sam Horne [Sam Hon, a laundryman on Gurley Street in the 1880 census] went down there one day, and tooted his horn in the ear of the damsel, who jumped into his wagon, and rode with him to Prescott, to the great disgust of her several Wickenburg husbands, but more especially to Ah-Own, the dreamy Chinaman who claimed her as his own. Well, Mr. Horne, the female, and the white escort arrived here in good season, Horne and the woman lived together and swore by each other, until the discarded Wickenburger arrived in this camp and commenced playing little games, the object of which was to get possession of his "wifey". To settle the question, Ah-Own appealed to the officers of the law, when the case was tried before recorder Ed. W. Wells, who, after hearing the testimony on both sides, and all that the lawyers—Judge Carter and Frank Ayers—had to say, ordered Mr. Horne to return the China woman over to her first husband, Ah-Own, in as good condition as he (Horne) had found her. This, too, after Horne had been married to So-So, or So-Sing—have forgotten her right name. Yielding, very reluctantly, to this distasteful decree, the female accompanied Ah-Own and party to headquarters at their wash-house, where, not liking the smell of the soapsuds, she screamed for her dear Horne, who, with his party, was about to freeze on to her, when Sheriff Thomas came up, escorted the female and male Chinaman to the recorder's office where Judge Wells tested the woman's love, and finding that it flowed in the direction of Sam Horne's horn spoon, permitted her to go 'mit Sam, who, at this writing, is in jail, serving a term of imprisonment for assaulting the sheriff.

We had almost forgotten to state that Judge Otis came nigh marrying the woman to another Chinaman; also, that upon being asked if she would take a (Sam) Horne for her lawful husband, she replied, in mingled Chinese and Californian, "You bet-tee."[51]

---

51. *Arizona Weekly Miner*, February 15, 1873.

In 1874 a woman who quite probably was Prescott's first Chinese prostitute made her appearance (Figure 6). Her loose-fitting silk pants outfit, groomed chignon, thin eyebrows, and rice-powdered face were typical of her class, although the reporter announcing her arrival was unaware of her occupation.

> Wickenburg stage arrived at about half past six, Thursday evening, with several passengers, and seven packs of mail. Among the passengers was a Chinese female, the first that has ever visited this town, and section of country, and, we hope, the last.[52]

By 1880, there were four more Chinese singsong girls at work beside Euro-Americans and Hispanics in the red-light district that had grown up along the corner of Granite and Goodwin streets adjacent to Chinese roominghouses. All the women indicated they were married, and one still lived with her husband. Probably they had been purchased by prospective mates, only to be resold as the opportunity presented itself. Since three thousand dollars was a common going rate, the temptation was strong for dealing in females.[53] The local singsong girls were under the supervision of Ah Yong, a thirty-five-year-old brothel operator assumed to have been a member of one of the west-coast tongs that controlled the Chinese prostitution racket.[54] Organized crime had come to Prescott.

In a few years child slavery had arrived as well. As background, it should be noted that in times of severe need Chinese peasant families considered female offspring more a liability than an asset. They were routinely disposed of. During the demoralizing crises of the nineteenth century, Chinese female infanticide may have ranged as high as seventy percent.[55] Hundreds of other young girls were sold into slave gangs brought surreptitiously into the United States. Pre-teens were used as domestics until they had matured enough to engage in sexual acts. The situation had become so deplorable that in 1871 the Methodist Church opened an asylum in San Francisco, and in 1873 the Presbyterian Woman's Occidental Board of Foreign Missions launched a campaign for the rescue of these youngsters. One child beyond their reach turned up in Prescott.

52. *Arizona Weekly Miner*, March 11, 1874.
53. Dillon 1962: 231.
54. U.S. Federal Census, Arizona Territory, 1870.
55. Wegars 1984.

[Figure 6] If the 1878 date on this photograph taken by Prescott pioneer, D. F. Mitchell, is correct, the unidentified woman portrayed likely was one of the town's first Granite Street prostitutes. All five Chinese women listed in the 1880 census plied that occupation. Her modest costume of full brocade tunic and black trousers indicates that she, like the local Chinese men, was of low social class. The fan and silk handerchief she holds, the jewelry and cosmetics she wears, and the unelaborated hair arrangement were standard attributes. Although footbinding did not become illegal until 1912, most probably her feet were not bound, since that was a custom restricted to females of higher status. *Courtesy* Sharlot Hall Museum.

[Figure 7] June Wong, victim of the tragic traffic in child slavery, ran away from her Prescott Chinese master. She was rescued by the T. W. Otis family, who legally adopted her and oversaw her education as a Christian, with the goal of allowing her to return to China as a missionary. *Courtesy* Sharlot Hall Museum.

She was June Wong (Figure 7). Fearing for her safety, June ran away from her Chinese "foster father," a local resident, to be taken in by Theodore W. Otis and his wife. Otis had driven into town in

1874 with a freight wagon load of groceries with which he opened a store. In addition to running this enterprise for three and a half decades, at various times he also served as postmaster and district court judge and was active in founding the Presbyterian and Congregational churches.[56] No doubt he was aware of the efforts being made in California to help victims like June. Eventually legally adopted by the Otis couple, June Wong worked as a servant in their household. Her wages went to educate her as a missionary so that in due time she could return to China on the church's behalf.

In addition to actively supporting prostitution, the Chinese were habitual gamblers. This form of recreation may have especially flourished in America because of the circumstances surrounding the sojourns.[57] In the back rooms of their temporary Chinatowns as well as in more formal gambling parlors, with time on their hands and a consuming eagerness to make a quick fortune, they enjoyed fantan, dominoes, checkers, a lottery called *pak hop piu*, and similar diversions.[58] Fantan, a game in which participants bet on the number of objects from one to four a dealer put in a container, was a favorite social affair.

There is just one record of a Chinese-run gambling parlor in Prescott, but along with most of the male Euro-American residents, the Chinese also frequented Prescott's many public gaming tables. Poker was preferred in those places. As noted by the *Enterprise*, March 27, 1886, "the Chinese are good patrons of all games of chance."

In March 1880, Prescott imposed a gambling tax of fifteen dollars. If no license was obtained, offenders were subject to a fine of twenty-five to three hundred dollars.[59] Very shortly, the local Chinese were in trouble.

> The celestial portion of our inhabitants were congregated this afternoon at the office of Justice A. O. Noyes, at which place some of their forces were being tried for the offense of carrying on gambling without a license. Capt. Hargrave appeared for the prisoners.[60]

56. Obituary, Archives, Sharlot Hall Museum.
57. Culin 1891: 14.
58. Culin 1890b: 196.
59. Village of Prescott, Ordinances, No. 21. Archives, Sharlot Hall Museum.
60. *Arizona Weekly Miner*, April 2, 1880.

The most pernicious habit the Chinese brought with them to America was the use of opium. The drug was obtained from the dried juice of the poppy *Papaver somniferum*, which was processed, rolled into balls, graded for several qualities, and packed into small, flat, brass tins. For centuries known in China for medicinal purposes, opium gained widespread popularity among all levels of society with the sixteenth-century introduction of tobacco. The two substances were smoked together to produce a state of dreamy euphoria. Soon opium was being used alone and proving particularly addictive. The British generally are considered responsible for encouraging the drug's demoralizing use because opium harvested in their holdings in India was a critical commodity in the large-scale trade for Chinese tea.

Recognizing the physical, emotional, and moral ravages among the populace caused by opium, in 1796, 1813, 1814, and 1839 the Chinese government outlawed its importation from regions such as India and tried to suppress its cultivation and use at home.[61] The collusion of smugglers, administrative officials, the producing British colonial empire, and Chinese addicts and pushers prevented eradication of the underground trade. In 1858 opium again was legalized owing to the badly needed high revenues involved. Chinese merchants openly dispatched the drug to overseas Chinese outlets. The first shipment of fifty-two boxes of opium reached San Francisco in 1861 on the ship *Ocean Pearl* out of Hong Kong.[62] In 1880 raw gum opium and opium prepared for smoking, together valued at more than one and a half million dollars, passed through United States Customs.[63] Once in the country, it was under the control of the various fighting tongs parlaying its distribution into high-stakes power and profit.

Like every other Chinese settlement in the West, Prescott had one or more opium dens. They were not the dark holes of iniquity the press made them out to be but were merely bare frame rooms behind a couple of grubby stores or washhouses on south Granite Street. Undoubtedly cramped and filthy, they were the dismal homes-away-from-home of some of the local Chinese. In their privacy, for many reasons that may be presumed to have included

61. Gernet 1982: 534.
62. Dillon 1962: 61.
63. Kane 1976: 16.

monotony, alienation, tension, or physical disabilities, some residents found relief or languor in the debilitating opium fumes.

The way in which this narcotic was consumed contributed to non-users' vague suspicions of indecency, for an opium smoke was not a loud convivial affair in a public place. The procedure began by lying on one's side, which, of course, dictated certain surroundings. A bed of sorts and semidarkness provided the right atmosphere. Then, on a long metal needle, one took a bit of the prepared, syrupy opium mass from its brass container, held it over the flames of a kerosene lamp until it bubbled, rolled it into a tiny pea, and forced it into the small hole of the warmed, flat-topped, ceramic bowl of a long-stemmed pipe. A deep drag produced an immediate peaceful sensation. Several further pipesful sometimes led to stupor.

Although agitated Euro-American neighbors were disgusted at what they thought went on in the dens, for a time they tolerated them as a Chinese eccentricity. After all, there were wide-open liquor parlors just a block away where a segment of the host society was similarly addicted to whiskey. The Euro-Americans likely also were cognizant of the problems some soldiers had experienced as an aftermath of the Civil War, when opium used recklessly as an ingredient in morphine, codeine, and patent medicines had created dependencies.[64] Regardless, it remained for the seduction of local innocents to bring the citizenry to attention. Out to make money any way possible and many themselves being users, the Chinese did not consider the supplying of opium to Euro-Americans as anything irregular. Outraged, strait-laced citizens thought differently. Matters began to come to a head before the end of the 1870s.

> Among the many evils and vices which the influx of Mongolian immigration has brought to the shores of the Pacific one of the worst is, without doubt, the detestable habit of opium-smoking, which is slowly and steadily growing upon our youths of both sexes. . . . Prescott being a live town, anxious to adopt all the innovations of the age, both good and bad, could not be long without its opium smoking. It was necessary for its proper growth and standing among the towns of the Pacific coast that it should have a half-lighted, stifling rookery, presided over by a cadaverous-looking heathen, in

64. Dai 1964: 645.

which our "way up" boys and fast young men—and we are sorry to say, representatives of the other sex—might waste away their money and their brains by puffing away at a drag, which would turn their stomach were it prescribed by a physician; but then you know "it's the fashion, and you ain't a sport if you can't stand a half dozen pipes of opium." Many of our citizens would be astonished to see the number of men and women who visit these Granite Street hovels, at all hours of the day and night, and if they want to satisfy themselves of the correctness of our assertions let them take a stand for a few hours at the corner of Granite and Goodwin streets. They will see hurrying in, stealthily, quite a number of habitees [*sic*] of both sexes, from some of our leading citizens down to the lowest harlot who plies her vocation on that street, and if they can manage to be passed in they will be able to feast their eyes with the disgusting sight of this powerful narcotic. Something should be done to stop this detestable failing, which seems to possess such enticing qualities.

The Chinese dens of Prescott carry on quite an extensive business in the way of opium smoking. There are several persons, not altogether Chinese in nationality, who pay for the privilege of inhaling the intoxicating fumes from opium pipes in the celestial dens of Prescott.[65]

Finally, in 1880, the authorities took action against those who provided the drug and bunks and those who took advantage of the service.

Any person who shall hereafter, within the corporate limits of the Village of Prescott, keep or maintain, or become an inmate of, or shall in any way contribute to the support of any place, house or room, where opium is smoked, or where persons assemble for the purpose of smoking opium or inhaling the fumes thereof, shall be declared guilty of a misdemeanor and shall be fined in the sum of not less than ten or more than one hundred dollars.[66]

65. *Enterprise*, August 13, 1877; *Arizona Weekly Miner*, October 24, 1879.
66. Village of Prescott, Ordinances, No. 22. Archives, Sharlot Hall Museum.

Even so, the practice of opium smoking continued.

> Ah Jim [a cook in the 1880 census] the Chinaman arrested
> yesterday for selling opium, and also for keeping an opium
> fumigating den, was tried before a jury in Recorder Rush's
> Court, found guilty as charged, and sentenced to pay a fine of
> $25 or serve 12½ days in the City Calaboose. Other cases of a
> similar nature will come up on Saturday.

> Dodson has several Chinese gentlemen in limbo for an in-
> fringement of a certain City ordinance prohibiting the smok-
> ing of opium within the city limits.[67]

At that point, a prominent lawyer who had made a specialty of
defending the civil rights of the immigrants contested the legality of
the ordinance.

> Judge Hargrave, counsel for the Chinese prisoner, charged
> with violating a city ordinance in regard to the use of opium,
> swore out a warrant and caused the arrest of City Recorder C.
> B. Rush and City Marshal J. M. Dodson this morning, for
> violation of Chinese rights and for overreaching their official
> duties. They were taken before Justice Noyes, and upon their
> petition the case was postponed until to-morrow morning or
> Saturday. There seems to be a difference of opinion in regard
> to the constitutionality of the Opium Ordinance.[68]

Apparently, Hargrave lost the argument; the ordinance was reissued
three years later, with the fine raised to three hundred dollars and a
possible penalty added of one year's imprisonment.

In 1887 the United States Congress passed an act prohibiting the
importation of opium for other than medical purposes. Laws or
not, opium smoking went unchecked, as was noted in the *Prescott
Weekly Courier* of February 17, 1893.

> Night before last Constable Miller, with the aid of two cit-
> izens, raided a Chinese opium joint of middle Granite Street,
> capturing twelve opium smokers, four pipes, and several cans
> of opium. There were three whites and nine Chinamen cap-

67. *Arizona Weekly Miner*, June 4, 1880.
68. Ibid.

tured. Thirteen persons were in the room at the time of the raid, but one got away. The constable states that when the room was entered the fiends were all lying in bunks arranged around the walls, one above another, and each prisoner was in a stupefied state until they had walked a short distance in the open air. They were brought before Judge Noyes, who held them in $50 bail each, trial to take place before him at 10 o'clock tomorrow. A white man and woman gave the bail and were released. The other ten prisoners went to jail.

Leading Chinamen rustled around all day yesterday and finally gave bonds for their opium-smoking brethren in jail, who were released about 6 o'clock last evening.

The following year nine Chinese were arrested for the same offense.[69] They pleaded guilty and were fined $22.85.

Other communities and states likewise were clamping down on opium users. On the international scene, public sentiment mounted against the havoc caused by the drug. Chinese rulers imposed a heavy tax on opium and secured a treaty with the British, in which the latter agreed to decrease their exports from India to China. Health conferences encouraged greater worldwide surveillance to curtail smuggling. All these efforts helped reduce, but not eliminate, the opium menace. The dens of Prescott remained local fixtures.

A recreational activity not usually considered in relation to the overseas Chinese was drinking. At home Chinese males were known to have been heavy users of alcoholic beverages of high potency and to have enjoyed drinking games and clubs.[70] It might be thought that in America, as with the Euro-Americans, social consumption of wines, brandy, or whiskey was another pleasure in which they indulged. However, eyewitness descriptions of nineteenth-century western life frequently mentioned the sobriety of the Chinese, with the implication that liquor was something they did not consume. In the boozy milieu of the frontier the drinking habits of the Chinese may not have been extraordinary enough to warrant comment, or

---

69. Register of Criminal Actions, Third Judicial District Court, Proceedings, June 1894, Yavapai County Court House.

70. Chang 1977: 278.

perhaps their imbibing was done within the privacy of Chinatown. That extensive drinking did occur has been suggested by archaeological research carried out in the last several decades in areas formerly occupied by Chinese. Quantities of globular stoneware spirits bottles of a type still made in China, as well as discarded glass American liquor and beer containers, have been unearthed. It should be noted that there was only one term in Chinese for alcoholic beverage. That was *pai chiu*, usually translated as "wine" but actually more closely resembling vodka in being distilled, made from a starch base such as sorghum, millet, or rice, and ninety-five to one hundred proof.[71] Some Chinese merchants in Prescott purchased other spirits from a local white wholesaler.

The Prescott Chinese also continued to be Chinese in several recreational celebrations that intrigued the Euro-American community. These included seasonal religious and social festivals commencing in the second-story hall on Granite Street but always spilling out into the surrounding neighborhood. No matter the occasion, the accompanying deafening noise from fusillades of exploding strings of firecrackers and what to western ears was exotic, discordant music provided by gong, drum, cymbals, and flute could not have failed to attract the attention of the whole town. The most elaborate celebration was that commemorating Chinese New Year.[72] This was primarily a social event but had religious overtones. An early description follows.

> People living within hearing of the Chinese quarters, need not be told, this morning, that China New Year began at midnight last night. Such another pandemonium as was maintained all along the line, from two o'clock until daylight, is not often heard in this well organized Christian land.
>
> Pistols, bombs, fire-crackers, in short, everything they could command, that would make a noise, was brought into requisition.
>
> This morning the whole China male population went out making New Year's calls, dressed in silk attire, and we ob-

71. Chang 1977: 342.
72. Chinese New Year was on the first moon after the sun entered the sign of Aquarius, therefore never earlier than January 21 or later than February 19.

served that in front of some of their residences they had difficulty in wading through the husks from bursted fire-crackers.

The fire-cracker business is a dangerous nuisance, and although it may be a part of their religion, as a means of frightening away the Devil, it is at the same time a source of many conflagrations, and ought to be a subject of police regulation.[73]

As inventors of gunpowder, the Chinese expectedly were fond of firecrackers and used them exuberantly. These noisemakers, laced into strings, were routinely included in stocks shipped from the west coast. If carelessly used, they did pose a threat to the huddle of frame buildings that already had experienced cyclic fires and re-erections. After 1880 the village council required a permit from the mayor before fireworks could be ignited, with noncompliance carrying a fine of ten to one hundred dollars. The penalty later was raised to three hundred dollars.[74]

The serving of special foods was an essential part of all the observances, even those carried out in the most removed corners of the Chinese world such as that at Prescott. Hospitable and with a gnawing but unacknowledged longing to be accepted, as well as reaffirming their own ethnicity to the world at large, Chinese of all economic levels opened many of their festive indulgences to whomever would join in. The Chinese labor class did not fully comprehend the distinctiveness of its cuisine on these occasions, since it took its way of life for granted. The local paper noted:

> Visitors will be welcome, and will be served with bird nest soup, shark's fins, fish maws, chop suey, Chinese candies, and many other concoctions strange to the American tastes.[75]

A week later the paper provided a fuller account:

> Inside the Joss House the stranger, no matter of what nationality, was welcomed, treated to choice Chinese delicacies, and sent on his way with the "Kong Hae Fat Tsi" greeting. The decorations in the Chinese house of worship were elaborate. Chinese lanterns hung everywhere, crimson silk draperies

73. *Arizona Weekly Miner*, February 1, 1878.
74. Village of Prescott, Ordinances. Archives, Sharlot Hall Museum.
75. *Arizona Journal Miner*, February 1, 1908.

hid the otherwise bleak walls, scrolls of Chinese prophecies and sayings of Confucius were profusely scattered about, and myriads of lighted candles and burning punk and incense lent aid to the air of orientalism which pervaded the place.

On one side of the big room, at the end of which stood the Chinese altar, adorned by the immobile Joss, the Chinese musicians were seated, all wearing hats or some other head covering, as did the visitors who entered from time to time, in groups of three and four, to stand chatting awhile, discussing the music which struggled, piecemeal from the several performers, and then to go on to the "Noodle Joint", where Chinese refreshments awaited them.[76]

Because Chinese music was not harmonious and the instruments used to produce it were unfamiliar, Euro-American observers frequently commented upon performances of Chinese bands at ceremonial functions. It is unknown whether music was also a form of entertainment when the sojourners gathered socially.

Occasions such as the New Year's festivities were attended by Euro-American townsmen, as the paper noted, but there is no clue that the Prescott Chinese ever were similarly invited to Euro-American civic or social functions. Some of what the Euro-Americans regarded as Chinese clannishness obviously resulted from their own thoughtlessness. Such rejection, whether intentional or not, surely served to drive the sojourners deeper into their own ethnicity in defense against psychological damage. Had families been permitted to join these men, it is possible that Euro-American rebuff would not have produced such self-defeating reaction.

THE CHINESE ARE ENTRENCHED

At the end of the 1870s the Prescott Chinese population had increased from the original six men to ninety-six males and five females, according to the federal census.[77] Population figures relative to Chinese are only suggestive because of the extreme fluidity of this group. A few men settled in for decades interspersed with home

---

76. *Arizona Journal Miner*, February 8, 1908.
77. U.S. Federal Census, Arizona Territory, 1870.

Table 1. Occupations of Chinese Residing in Territorial Prescott

Occupation	1880	1900	1910
laundryman	30	61	40
cook	17	72	53
domestic servant	14	1	1
gardener	14	6	9
laborer	10	37	3
merchant	2	10	7
restaurant keeper	2	2	8
restaurant worker	—	24	—
waiter	1	6	5
dishwasher	1	1	1
clerk	1	—	2
miner	1	—	3
brothel keeper	1	—	—
prostitute	5	1	—
peddler	—	4	—
hotel proprietor	—	1	1
contractor	—	1	—
woodchopper	—	1	—
shoemaker	—	1	—
porter	—	—	1
delivery man	—	—	1
Total	99	229	135

Source: U.S. Federal Census, Arizona Territory

visits to China, but the majority were rootless, restive, unburdened by worldly goods, and drifted from place to place, job to job. Nevertheless, records reveal that in 1880 there was just one married couple in the Prescott colony. They were Ah Chung, a cook, and Chow Aie, a prostitute. They lived on Granite Street with Ah Can, a miner. All the immigrants had been born in their homeland, but no data on their prior length of stay in the United States are available. They ranged from fifteen to sixty-two years of age and worked at thirteen different low-level vocations. Not one was unemployed. Nor was one of what might be considered a professional, white-collar class. Laundering was by far the most common occupation, but cooking also engaged a sizable percentage of the immigrants (Table 1). Some participants in these trades counted on advertising to bring in Euro-American customers, indicating one kind of adjustment to circumstances the Chinese were ready to make.

Wong Lee, all same Melicano [American] man, runs the wash house near the foot bridge at the crossing of Granite Creek. Call and see his laundry and procure one of his cards, printed in American after the style of the 19th century.

Table 2. Places of Chinese Residence in Prescott

Location	1880	1900	1910
Granite Street	46	37	128
Montezuma Street	28	119	5
Gurley Street	9	6	5
Cortez Street	1	11	—
Goodwin Street	1	18	5
Willis Street	—	4	—
Whipple Barracks	10	—	5
Miller Valley	10?	—	8

Source: U.S. Federal Census, Arizona Territory

> New Restaurant, Open Monday, February 3. Ah Wah, late
> cook at the Cabinet, has rented the Dining Rooms attached to
> P. M. Fisher's Saloon, where by good cooking and attention to
> business, he hopes to merit a share of the public patronage.
> Board per week, $8.00; Single meals .50. Chicken and eggs
> three times a week.[78]

Servants, gardeners, and laborers comprised the next most numerous groupings. All five women were prostitutes. The youngest
two were twenty years old; the eldest was forty-five.

Almost half of the Asians lived on two blocks of Granite Street,
confirming that it was their principal quarter (Table 2). Ten had
found employment and lodging at Whipple Barracks. Twenty-eight
others roomed either at the rear of the restaurant-saloon complex
along Montezuma Street or in an upstairs boardinghouse there.

No address is indicated in the 1880 census for ten of those engaged full time in gardening (Figure 8). It is believed they likely
had begun to develop vegetable plots, predictably known as the
Chinese Gardens, at the north end of Granite Street across from the
confluence of Granite and Miller creeks, and resided in several huts
near them. In this locality, the pine-clad hills flattened out into
gravelly terraces suitable for small-scale farming. Four other gardeners are noted as dwelling on Granite and Montezuma streets.
Either they walked the short distance to their out-of-town fields or
they cared for kitchen plots located around some of the Chinese-
occupied buildings or Euro-American gardens within the settlement
proper.

78. *Arizona Weekly Miner*, April 2, 1880.

[Figure 8] Substituting horses and mules for the water buffalo they had used in South China to pull hand plows, Chinese gardeners filled a critical need on the Arizona frontier for fresh vegetables and fruits. By 1880 ten gardeners, such as this unidentified man, already were at work in the vicinity of Prescott. *Courtesy* Sharlot Hall Museum.

These Chinese had seen another need in the economic network of the town and were alert enough to take advantage of it. Home gardens were sufficient only for individual families, and Prescott's removal from major transportation routes made it difficult to procure any substantial amounts of fresh produce for commercial use or for the military messes. In this instance, the Chinese had the benefit of an agrarian heritage extending back four thousand years to the rise of the Neolithic. From that time on, labor-intensive manual farming had brought most of the arable eastern Asian continent under control and had fed millions. Intimate knowledge of soils, plants, and microclimates became the aggregate legacy of generations of land-bound masses. It was a priceless fund of knowledge upon which local Chinese could draw.

It was the older elements of the Chinese community in Prescott who turned to agriculture as a means to their common end. Perhaps their age made them less adaptable to taking on new trades. At any rate, on the outskirts of the village they broke virgin sod, hauled off boulders, weeded, put down wells because the nearby creeks ran only during summer showers, and sowed the vegetable and fruit crops familiar to Euro-Americans. Had they followed their ancient method of using nightsoil as fertilizer, there surely would have been howls of protest from horrified observers, as in California.[79] The common products were brought by one-horse wagon to be sold primarily to the town's eating establishments. Since many of those restaurants and boardinghouse kitchens were operated by country-men, it was a distribution chain from Chinese gardener to Chinese cook to Euro-American consumer. Chinese vegetables, such as bok choy, snow peas, winter melons, or long, hot, white radishes, sup-plied their own ethnic group. Very possibly the men also raised hogs and chickens for the same clients.

The cooks provided services using American products for the dominant Euro-American society and therefore were on the front lines of cultural interaction. The washermen and gardeners were less so. However, the two merchants and one clerk counted in the 1880 census functioned exclusively within Chinatown. As ethnic en-trepreneurs, they moved in to establish businesses geared to the needs felt by the local Chinese for maintaining their homeland pattern of living as much as possible. Probably they never bothered to learn English because both their suppliers and customers com-municated in Chinese, and they had no set prices since bargaining was the norm in their experience. Use of United States currency was essential for business conducted with Euro-Americans, but there is some evidence that coins minted in China in small denominations circulated within the overseas Chinese enclaves.[80] The ageless abacus, its bells clicking rapidly along vertical wires, was more effi-cient than an adding machine for the Chinese merchants. There may have been some specialization in inventories. To judge from better-known circumstances in similar communities, the cramped, dingy Chinese stores, filled with odors unfamiliar to most westerners, were crammed to the rafters with an amazing variety of foodstuffs, spices, teas, wine, herbal medicines, culinary herbs, tobacco, clay pipes, opium paraphernalia, paper and silk lanterns, musical instru-ments, playing cards and wooden or ivory counters, candles, joss sticks, double-edged wooden combs, baskets of various sizes, hard-

79. Spier 1958: 81.
80. Greenwood 1980: 113–23; Olsen 1983: 118.

ware, clothes, kitchen gear, soup spoons, and serving dishes. Perhaps even more important than the familiar articles from China was the role of the store as a place where Chinese men could congregate to discuss the events of their day, much as Euro-American colleagues were doing in other emporiums. For the illiterate, the shopkeeper may have served as a scribe, writing occasional letters to families across the ocean.

In a few years a third shopkeeper had arrived. He, too, opened a store in the Chinese quarter, but it is obvious he hoped to sell some of his imported stock of both Chinese and Japanese derivation to Euro-American residents. The *Arizona Journal Miner*, October 9, 1889, reported,

> Queng Sing, the enterprising Chinese crockery and tea merchant on Granite Street has just received a large invoice of elegant flowered china wares from the land of Confucius. Also a lot of pure Orlang tea, which will be sold cheap.[81]

Of the minorities in Prescott in 1880, the Chinese were only slightly less numerous than the 114 Hispanics. Among the latter was a soldier at Whipple Barracks with a wife and six children, as well as six other families residing in town. It is not known whether there was any intermingling of Chinese and Hispanics, as there was occasionally in Tucson. The third group, blacks, was made up of five men, two women, and one child. Although all these social components were of low economic status, the men generally did not compete for jobs. Indicative of the important freight connection to Sonora and California, half of the men with Spanish surnames were teamsters. The two other jobs frequently filled by Hispanics were those of laborers and miners. The rest worked at blacksmithing, herding, farming, or cutting wood. The black men were laborers, cook, circus rider, and jockey. It was the minority women who, through taking in washing or peddling sex, edged in on the Chinese job market.

All overseas Chinese automatically belonged to two associations.[82] One was made up of clan members with the same surname. The other comprised those who had originated in the same village

81. Oolong tea is a semifermented green variety.
82. Light 1972: 81–83; Lyman 1974.

or region in southern China and spoke the same dialect. Both bodies provided moral support and social services for their members, at the same time serving to reinforce their cultural identity. Bonds of family and territory had held Chinese society together for millennia, and even in the extenuating circumstances of residence in the New World, they provided the glue for ethnic continuity. Therefore, some Euro-American observers saw the associations as an obstacle to Chinese acculturation.[83]

In the 1850s, a super-organization of six of these district organizations evolved rapidly to become the political voice for the sojourners. Called the Six Companies by nineteenth-century Euro-Americans, its modern name is the Chinese Consolidated Benevolent Association. It represented the Chinese in legal matters or labor disputes, provided for the ill, loaned money, operated recreational centers, and cared for the dead.[84] Additionally, there were fraternal organizations made up of persons from families or districts too small to have much influence. Because the larger district associations ruthlessly limited participation in certain trades to their own members, these lesser groups degenerated into the infamous tongs, whose route to power and money was through various illegal enterprises, such as gambling, opium peddling, and prostitution. Membership in the tongs was open to any Chinese regardless of family or place of origin, but for many it meant a life outside the law. The most savage came to be known as hatchetmen: to defend the turf of their particular tongs, they often fought with cleaver-like swords.[85]

It is uncertain which specific clan or district-dialect associations existed among the Prescott Chinese, but lineages are suggested by the five most common surnames: Kee, Lee, Yee, Fong, and Chung. Customarily, members of each surname grouping addressed each other as "cousin" and felt obliged to offer mutual social, moral, and employment support and to stand together against any usurpation of their positions by rival clans.[86] Often they lived and worked together, as in the case of two Lees at 245 South Montezuma Street, two other Lees at 226 West Gurley Street, and two Kees at 130 South Granite Street.[87] Most, if not all, these immigrants had

83. Lee 1960: 148.
84. Weisberger 1970: 218.
85. Hoy 1942: 9.
86. Light 1972: 83.
87. U.S. Federal Census, Arizona Territory, 1900.

come to America from the Toishan district south of Canton, the area that contributed the greatest percentage of overseas Chinese. The Sze Yap dialect was spoken by these people, who were regarded by more cultured Cantonese as humble provincials most likely to have engaged in laundering, small-scale retailing, or cooking.[88] Their association was the Ning Yeung Company, formed in 1854 after separating from the Sze Yap parent organization, whose purposes were similar or complementary to those of the surname associations.[89] In a small community such as Prescott, it is possible that either the lineage or the district organizations were lacking. Such a gap would not have reduced the group's homogeneity, which was based upon social structure transferred from China.

The documented secret society in Prescott was the Chee Kung Tong, better known to Euro-Americans as the Chinese Masons or the Triad Society. Also called I'hing, it was a worldwide organization with a chapter established in San Francisco in 1863.[90] From there, it spread to nearly all Chinese communities throughout the West. The Chee Kung Tong had no relationship with Freemasonry as it was known to Euro-Americans, other than secret oaths and similar rituals, but had begun primarily as a politically oriented body that functioned as a popular voice against the Manchus.[91] However, criminal elements soon penetrated the society, giving rise to the notorious fighting tongs as splinter groups broke away. The Chee Kung Tong set itself up as an underground government for the Chinese. It provided mutual aid or protection to its members, frequently by violent means. It also assumed some of the duties of the Six Companies in seeing to proper funerals and taking leadership in dealing with the non-Asian world outside of Chinatown. Some sociologists have suggested that Sze Yap men more readily joined this society because their ignorance and poverty made them vulnerable to oppression.[92] In Prescott the joss house, or meeting hall, likely was maintained by the Chee Kung Tong, which claimed a membership of eighty percent of the local Chinese colony.[93]

---

88. Dillon 1962: 83; Lee 1960: 146.
89. Light 1972: 140.
90. Culin 1890a: 42; 1970; Lee 1960: 168.
91. Dillon 1962: 54;. Lyman 1970: 39.
92. Culin 1970: 3.
93. *Arizona Journal Miner*, April 14, 1909.

These various associations offered the Chinese a united front for coping with Euro-American Prescott with their legendary inscrutability. Beneath that seemingly impassive facade, however, seething internal disharmony from time to time erupted into disturbances of the peace and eventual conflicts with the law.[94]

Within a few years after the Chinese had infiltrated the California mother lode, trouble brewed between them and Euro-Americans seeking the same quick rewards. At the same time, virulent Euro-American resentment occasionally led to gang skirmishes, but there was no organized threat by Euro-Americans against their perceived competitors. What seems to have been desired was Chinese segregation into jobs that no one else wanted. Fortuitously, in the middle 1860s the potential for ugly fights was short-circuited by the siphoning away of thousands of Chinese laborers for railroad construction. But once the first major transcontinental line was completed with Chinese manpower, many Euro-American workers from the east coast poured back over it into California. Once again, they were pitted against the Chinese, who came in ever-increasing numbers as a result of the Burlingame Treaty, which gave them the right of unrestricted immigration, freedom of religion, and access to education. Frustrated Euro-Americans turned to "America for Americans" as a battle cry, although there was no concise idea of just who, other than Anglo Saxons, qualified. Racism was equated with Americanization.

Anti-Chinese attitudes turned into mob violence and hoodlumism. News of these disturbances soon reached the Arizona Territory from California, where the Los Angeles Chinese quarter had been burned to the ground and nineteen inhabitants killed.[95] While supportive of the Euro-American cause, a local observer pointed out that circumstances were different in Prescott.

> The white laborers of California, and their friends, are now red-hot upon the subject of cheap labor, as represented by the thousands of Chinese in that State. F. M. Pixley, Rev. Father Buchard and scores of others keep a pitching into the Johns, with little or no effect, we presume. Here, in Arizona, discussion of the question of cheap labor is hardly in order. True, we

94. Lyman 1974: 22.
95. Lyman 1970: 23.

have some few Chinese, but they have a strong desire to get all they can for their labor and spend it. We, nevertheless, sympathize with our California brethren, and think that they and their State would be better off if there were no heathen Chinese to bother.[96]

Five years later Prescott reporters took another look at the troubles over the Chinese and had recommendations for solving some of the community woes resulting from their work and thrift ethics. The *Arizona Weekly Miner* commented,

All of these Chinese are steadily employed in various vocations, and their wages each can be safely put down per diem at $1, or about $2,000 per month. Thus it will be seen that even out here in a very remote corner of the globe the Celestials manage to get away with something like $24,000 per annum, the major part of which the few Chinese who live among us can ship away from the Territory $100,000, never more to be seen in this part of the world. It would be much better to invite poor white men and women who are starving in some of the large cities to come and partake of that which the Chinese rice-eaters and misers are reaping.[97]

This argument had several obvious points of weakness. First, estimations of Chinese savings likely were exaggerated. The flow of money out of the country undoubtedly was real, but the sojourners also pumped spendings back into circulation. Second, it had been shown repeatedly that the majority of the Euro-Americans shunned the menial labors into which the Chinese had been forced, and thus the issue of job competition was invalid. Moreover, living on the frontier, with its isolation and hardships, was not to everyone's liking, no matter whether rich or poverty stricken.

Not to be outdone in the running debate, the *Enterprise* added,

Several Chinese—perhaps 100 of them—have penetrated thus far into Arizona and established themselves in business here. They appear to be frugal and industrious. Many white people look on them as interlopers. They own and run several washhouses and are, it is said, doing a thriving business. White

96. *Arizona Weekly Miner*, March 22, 1873.
97. *Arizona Weekly Miner*, November 29, 1878.

workers derive but little benefit from their presence here: store-keepers ditto. They have their own store-keeper, and use mostly goods brought from China. As washermen, they have never had any mercy on white men and women's clothing. As house servants, many of them have too great a desire "to run things to suit themselves." Why, then, do not our people try to dispense with their services. No honest white men or women who have to labor for a living ought to be above doing honest, honorable labor. Why, then, not start one or two steam laundries here, white laboring men and women, and earn the money that now goes into heathen hands?[98]

This advice fell on deaf ears, although the previous year two Euro-American ladies had opened a hand laundry on the east side of Montezuma Street and advertised that they would call for and return laundry free.[99] Their effort may have failed; no further advertising appeared in the newspapers.

Meanwhile, on the west coast, drought, failed mining speculation, and economic depression provided the opportunity for demagogues to turn the hated Chinese into scapegoats. They were blamed for everything from natural disasters to the introduction of leprosy.[100] By the 1880s, the calls for their total exclusion by organized labor and national political parties had become louder. Suspicious westerners did not believe that their eastern fellow citizens fully understood the depth of the problem because as yet only a relatively few Chinese had moved across the continent, whereas in California there was a Chinese population of seventy-five thousand.[101] As a bill for Chinese exclusion was before Congress, the *Prescott Weekly Courier* editorialized,

> The press and people are taking the greatest interest in the Chinese question and the opposition to Miller's bill from eastern sources promises to make of it a sectional question unless some speedy settlement is reached. The fact that the large public meetings are everywhere being called on the coast to

98. *Enterprise*, December 4, 1878.
99. *Enterprise*, June 13, 1877.
100. *Arizona Weekly Miner*, June 20, 1879; *Prescott Weekly Courier*, September 2, 1882.
101. Clyde and Beers 1966: 158–59.

give urgency to the measures now pending is accepted as evidence that the opposition to the Pacific coast views of the Chinese question is developing unlooked for strength in the Atlantic states. The cause of the Chinaman is secretly if not openly opposed by the monopoly corporations of the coast, and it is said that the heavy eastern capitalists are yielding their co-operation to their Pacific coast conferees. . . . Numerically we constitute a small proportion of the population of the country, and a pro-Chinese sentiment promulgated and engineered by these so-called apostles of "liberal thought" is likely to awaken responses in the breasts of millions of people in whom the Chinese question is a simple abstraction and who activated by mistaken ideas of humanity may impose on us a perpetuation of the present status of the Chinaman. Let us hope that Miller's bill may speedily pass to the condition of a law and that the Chinamen may be buried beyond the hope of resurrection on our coast.

All accounts agree in stating that Chinese coolies are now shipped to the Pacific coast by the thousands. As people here have enough of them, we hope the bill stopping the shipping of any more of them for the next twenty years will soon become a law by a House passage and the President's signature. We want America for Americans and such Europeans as are willing to come here and become true Americans.

The coolie system, though differing in form, has identically the same political effect as African slavery. It makes a large proprietary class, excludes white labor, dominates and controls vast expanses of Territory, and is wholly sectional in its occupation of the soil.[102]

In spite of what some westerners considered Atlantic seaboard softness on the Chinese, the first Exclusion Act passed in 1882, thereby repudiating the Burlingame Treaty. The racial restriction that singled out the Chinese was insidious enough, but also unprecedented was the targeting of one discrete economic class. The new law stated that for ten years no additional Chinese laborers

102. *Prescott Weekly Courier*, March 11, 18, 1882; April 8, 1882.

were to be admitted to the United States. Included in this category with domestic servants, cooks, miners, farmers, and others who toiled for daily wages were the laundrymen, who had ascended to the very modest level of small businessmen. Those who operated restaurants or ran grocery or general merchandise outlets were considered admissable skilled labor, provided they had certain assets. Scholars and diplomats exempted from the ruling represented only a minute fraction of the incoming throng of immigrants and did not comprise an element of frontier society. All Chinese in the country as of 1882 could remain but were declared ineligible for citizenship. Under no circumstances could they bring alien wives into the United States. Over twenty thousand men caught on return trips to China found themselves barred from legal reentry, although supposedly a sojourner could return if he had a wife, child, or parent in the United States or property or savings worth one thousand dollars.[103]

The curtailment of Chinese immigration, which dropped to just 279 persons two years later,[104] did little to quiet the rampant clamor against the Asians already present. Press rhetoric grew more vitriolic and reckless. In addition to lack of tolerance for cultural and sociological differences, the Chinese were called slaves, a touchy issue in the post-Civil War climate. Actually, the Chinese had come to America voluntarily and, in fact, earlier had been eagerly invited. As was the case with European immigrants, they were the needy poor. They were regarded as job competitive, but some objective observers admitted the Chinese often performed better. Perhaps the Chinese accepted less pay because they were more desperate. Blocked from undertaking some types of work, they were said to have become parasitic, making money off Euro-Americans, never mind that it was in capacities that Euro-Americans disdained.

It was also argued that the Chinese did not help local economies. They traded with their own ethnic sources or, through frugality now interpreted as miserliness, sent most of their earnings out of the country. Prodigal Euro-Americans little realized that thrift and condemnation of waste were glorified Chinese values.[105] The Chinese left the United States periodically in order to visit their fam-

103. Perkins 1984: 217–32.
104. Tsai 1983: Table 1.
105. Dun 1965: 345.

ilies, sometimes causing minor disruptions in local services. A frequent complaint was that they paid no taxes, even though special levies against many of their endeavors amassed additional revenues. In 1883 the village council of Prescott joined other municipalities in enacting tax legislation aimed specifically at the Chinese. Article 9 of the local ordinances for that year read, "For keepers or owners of laundries or any place where washing or ironing is carried on for the public, ten dollars per quarter."[106] Chinese vices were considered repugnnant, notwithstanding parallel Euro-American participation in the same or comparable pastimes. It was claimed that the Asians did not want citizenship, but such status had been denied them by the United States Congress.

This cloud of misconception and protest led to severe rioting in all west-coast towns with a Chinese presence, twenty-five in California alone.[107] Inland, dozens of Chinese were murdered senselessly in Wyoming and Colorado, and others in various localities were driven out of lodgings and places of business.

In terms of Sinophobia, 1886 was a year of crisis in the Arizona Territory. Public agitation with incidents of violence occurred in the mining towns of Clifton, Tombstone, and Bisbee. Chinese railroad workers were attacked in Flagstaff. A committee of territorial businessmen urged Governor Zulick to prevent Chinese from engaging in commerce.

It is impossible to know how much anger residents of Prescott felt over the Chinese in their midst, but Stephen G. Marcou mounted a one-man campaign against them. A French immigrant who recently had come to Prescott by way of southern Arizona, he placed a series of letters to the editor in local papers. He proposed an Anti-Chinese League such as had been organized in the troubled mining camps.

> That a majority of the citizens of Yavapai do not want to encourage the immigration into the county of the Chinese who are being expelled from the Pacific coast is a fact so obvious that no arguments are needed to demonstrate it; but the best way to get rid of the heathens is the problem which should engage our attention.

106. Village of Prescott, Ordinances, No. 9. Archives, Sharlot Hall Museum.
107. Wei Min She Labor Committee 1974: 23.

The first thing to be done is to organize an anti Chinese League, composed of respectable citizens, every member of which shall pledge himself to obey the lawful mandates of a duly elected Executive Board; this will insure united and harmonious action without which little good can be affected.

Some of the measures which will probably be discussed by the Board and adopted, if after due consideration, they are deemed likely to advance the interests of the League, may be the following:

All members to patronize exclusively restaurants, boarding houses and hotels where no Chinese cooks or waiters are employed.

All members to abstain from voting for any office seekers who employ or deal with Chinese, or are known to sympathize with them.

The creation of a fund by small monthly contributions from each member of the League, to be used for encouraging the establishment of white laundries and other industries monopolized by the Mongols.

The Chinese have not yet gained such a foothold in our community as in some of the counties of the Pacific coast, and it is reasonable to expect that they can be got rid of with less trouble and by using less energetic means than have had to be used there.

The best time to abate a nuisance is when it is in its incipient stage and the Chinese are a nuisance in Yavapai.[108]

Although Marcou begrudgingly acknowledged that the Chinese had many admirable qualities, he pressed his case by using the common unsubstantiated arguments of the day.

With all due regard for those that think differently, I am of the opinion that much of our financial and moral depression which prevails in our midst, is in a degree due to the baneful influence of our Mongolian population, for, were it not for them we would retain more of the money put in circulation, more white independent homes would have been built up, and more lasting improvements made; our taxes would be lighter because we would have more taxpayers and more taxable property.

108. *Arizona Journal Miner*, March 21, 1886.

It is, I think, no exaggeration to say that more than $100,000 of our money has found its way to China, since the unlucky day that the first Chinaman was allowed to establish himself in our country. But what is of more moment than the loss of the money is the loss to us of probable improvements which would have been made by all the poor and industrious, white families, who have been driven off by Chinese competition.

True, the Chinese make better servants than the whites; they are more docile, more servile, and will put up with more arrogance; in fact, they are natural born slaves; but the slavery system has ruined more communities than it has built up. Chinamen pay their rents with more promptness than the whites, and for that very reason, lands rented to them are withdrawn from the real estate market. We want no Landlordism here for, next to slavery, it is the greatest curse of mankind. What we want are small independent homes which make every man and woman feel an interest in the welfare of the community in which they live.

To sum up, the presence of the Chinese among us has a tendency to make the rich richer and the poor poorer. Should the aristocrats of official [illegible], of finance, trade and speculation, succeed in retaining the Chinese in Yavapai County, they will eventually have to build poor houses for the whites.[109]

A public meeting at the courthouse resulted from Marcou's efforts. Several prominent citizens addressed the ideal of giving preference to Euro-American labor, but on a note of caution, all pleaded for more peaceful, lawful measures than had been taken elsewhere. No one was prepared to become involved in physical strife. A slate of officers was elected, with the outspoken journalist John H. Marion as president.[110] Future meeting dates were scheduled. The *Courier's* account of the new organization was appropriately moderate.

The Anti Chinese League of Prescott appears to mean busi-

109. *Arizona Journal Miner*, March 26, 1886.
110. Other league members were J. H. A. Marsh, I. P. Ingwerson, Michael Hickey, eEd. H. Cook, Charles O'Malley, Eugene Pannenberg, J. N. Rodenburg, and Walter Halligan. *Prescott Morning Courier*, March 26, 1886.

ness. As soon as 100 persons shall have signed the roll, business will be commenced in earnest. Harsh measures are not to be put in force, but the aim of the League will be to drive the Chinese from town and country by boycotting them and all who favor them with their patronage. Ample time will be given all who employ Chinese to procure other help and a steam laundry will, we hear, be started and run, so as to make washing anything but remunerative to the unwelcome fellows who now fatten upon its profits. The League will insist that Chinese gardeners must also go, since they are keeping white people from supplying our markets with vegetables. As for the Courier, it employs no Chinaman and does not propose to do so, and it hopes to see all their places occupied by white or colored people.[111]

Marcou countered with several suggestions, the most telling of which was a nineteenth-century chauvinistic approach guaranteed to make no friends among the women of Prescott.

As a possible solution to this knotty problem, various schemes are daily put forth; some say "boycott", others say "steam laundry"; the more philanthropic say, "women". The boycott is an aggressive process and will surely array against those who attempt to use it or open covert hostility of many courageous and intelligent men who might be persuaded, but will not yield to compulsion; boycotting should be used only as a last resort. The steam laundry may be a good thing; certainly preferable to Mongolian labor, but like an ice machine it takes some capitol to start one and it takes more brains and industry to run it successfully than is possessed by the average Smart Alex. Moreover it has proven a failure on the Pacific Coast, in competition with Chinese labor.

The women of Yavapai must solve the problem and they will do it if it is left to them; the women of Knob Hill can give preference to white help and the poor who live in less elevated positions will work willingly to help raise their growing children. Women are preferable to machines in domestic economy.[112]

111. Ibid. Usual estimates of laundry income are six to twelve dollars a month. Ong 1983: 73.

112. *Arizona Journal Miner*, April 13, 1886.

It was seven years before a steam laundry was established on the banks of Miller Creek next to the old city dam. Presumably, its owner was not the average Smart Alex. In the meantime, there were no indications that the women of Prescott were inspired to turn to commercial hand laundering. They could not compete with the two-dollar-per-dozen-shirt rate of the Chinese nor had inclination to try. Nevertheless, the papers put pressure on Euro-American employers to get on the anti-Chinese bandwagon, at the same time pinpointing a common fault attributed to Euro-American or Mexican workers.

> Chinese cooks in Prescott are receiving $75 per month and board, while Chinese house servants refuse to do any family washing while receiving a salary of $40 per month and board. This help would all be replaced with white labor if good reliable and sober help could be obtained.[113]

In response, the Pioneer Hotel advertised that it engaged only Euro-American employees. A new business called the White Laundry promisingly reported it had served thirty patrons in one week. Marcou himself ran advertisements on behalf of a Euro-American woman who wished to take in washing and a Euro-American man who sought a job as a camp cook. On March 30 he optimistically wrote,

> Good, steady white cooks, servant girls and washerwomen (to take the place of Chinese who are leaving Prescott) can now obtain work at good prices.[114]

It is particularly intriguing that at this very time Marcou personally opened a nursery business, obviously hoping to take advantage of an incipient pro-Euro-American mood and casting some doubt on his true intentions in the crusade against the Prescott sojourners. His advertisement read,

> The Prescott Garden. North end of McCormick street, offers for sale strong plants of rhubarb and asparagus, and of strawberry plants, which will bear fruit this season, onion sets, horseradish sets, double hollyhocks in four distinct colors which will bloom this season. These plants are raised by white

---

113. *Enterprise*, March 27, 1886.
114. *Arizona Journal Miner*, March 30, 1886.

labor and the money realized from their sale will not be withdrawn from circulation by being sent to China.[115]

Announcements of the Anti-Chinese League meetings and occasional editorials rehashing what had become the threadbare "Chinese problem" continued for the next several months, but by summer both ceased to be covered by the town's press. There had been no significant disruptions to the daily routines of the mountain community and no mass departures of the Chinese. There had been no pogroms, no autos-da-fé. Calmer, pragmatic Prescottonians apparently took stock of the situation and realized that the Chinese had become vital, perhaps irreplaceable, cogs in the societal system as it then existed.

Another clue to at least limited acceptance of the Chinese in Prescott is found in the publicity given Joe Ah Jew (Figure 9). In 1880, as a seventeen-year-old, he had arrived in town to make his fortune. Some records indicate that he already had lived in Arizona for six years. If so, he must have been a lad of eleven years or less when he departed from China. Once in Prescott, he went to work in one of the local eating establishments and within six years had become its manager. Moreover, he had learned to read and write English, had achieved proficiency in his trade, and had made a deliberate decision to be a settler rather than a sojourner. Joe Ah Jew became the first naturalized Chinese in the Arizona Territory. An 1884 Tucson newspaper told its readers of his status as a new citizen, a privilege granted by an independent-minded judge in defiance of a national law denying citizenship through naturalization for the Chinese, and noted that Joe Ah Jew had voted in an election in Prescott.[116] During the height of the Anti-Chinese League controversy, the *Enterprise* printed a brief item about this illustrious youth.

> Joe Ah Jew, a naturalized Chinese-American, who is well known through northern Arizona as a caterer, has charge of the culinary department of the Reception Restaurant. Joe has been in Arizona 14 years.[117]

115. *Arizona Journal Miner*, March 21, 1886.
116. *Arizona Star*, November 9, 1884.
117. *Enterprise*, April 20, 1886.

[Figure 9] Joe Ah Jew, photographed here about the turn of the century, distinguished himself as a Prescott caterer, restaurant owner, and Arizona's first Chinese naturalized citizen. Other than voting in elections, learning English, and becoming a Christian convert, his eagerness to blend into the American scene is reflected in his Western wardrobe, complete with flower in the lapel. However, in anticipation of home visits to China, he did not cut off his queue, shown wrapped over the crown of his head. Notwithstanding this apparent cultural adaptation over forty years residency, the laws prohibiting immigration of his family probably made him decide in 1919 to return permanently to his homeland. *Courtesy* Sharlot Hall Museum.

From that job Joe Ah Jew went on to a new challenge, as announced in an 1890 advertisement:

Ben Butler's Chop House. Montezuma Street, next door to Cob Web Saloon. Open all night. Meals Served at all hours. Fried Oysters and Game in Season and other things the market affords. Joe Ah Jew, Prop.[118]

The mild, short-lived fracas over the Prescott Chinese seemed to have cleared the air. Thereafter, fewer derogatory and more descriptive newspaper articles about the Chinese were printed. However, one brusque two-liner subtly exposed the raw underside of some lingering public opinion.

Chinese wash-house burns down; Chinaman perishes in flames; also a dog, cat, and a rattlesnake.[119]

The biggest news of the winter of 1891 was the flooding of Granite Creek, which threatened to take out a new footbridge and the railroad roundhouse. For three blocks through the part of town where most of the Chinese lived the normally placid, if not dry, stream had been converted into a raging torrent by unusual runoff (Map 3). Descriptions of the damage included two items that involved those residents.

About seven o'clock the kitchen of the Chinese wash house, near the ice factory, started on a voyage down stream, and the remainder of the building was so badly undermined that it now stands at an angle about forty-five degrees.

A new channel is also said to have been cut by the stream below town through the Chinese gardens. All occupants of the houses along McCormick Street above the bridge except one or two moved out to higher ground. Those on the west side of Granite Street between Gurley and Willis streets did the same thing.[120]

Otherwise, life just drifted along, with little other than the occasional gunfight or fisticuffs on Whiskey Row to break the monot-

118. *Arizona Weekly Miner*, 1890.
119. *Prescott Morning Courier*, February 1894.
120. *Arizona Journal Miner*, February 25, 1891.

[Figure 10] The Chinese New Year celebration was a time of open house at the Prescott joss house. Probably this picture portrays such an occasion during the 1890s, when the local Oriental population was at its peak and much of the anti-Chinese sentiment had faded. The mixture of individuals from several local ethnic groups posing for this photograph suggests a relaxed atmosphere. A number of Euro-American men and boys mingle with Chinese hosts; a black appears at the foot of the stairs.

By the end of the century, the Chinese men in Prescott had adopted Western attire. One gentleman in the lower center, with business suit, shirt, tie, and tan fedora, may have been a visiting tong dignitary from the west coast. Next to him is what appears to be one of the rare local Chinese families. As was usual, the wife retained her traditional costume. On the other side of the suited man is an elderly Chinese apparently filling the tiny bowl of a customary long-stemmed tobacco pipe. Just behind the flagpole is a Euro-American soldier, one of those stationed at Fort Whipple who was soon to be shipped out to the Spanish American War. Later, an American flag was to fly from that pole in appreciation for kind treatment extended to Chinese who aided American forces in Manila.

The first floor of the joss house had become a laundry, and was closed for the holiday. On the second floor, banners (probably red) with Chinese inscriptions appropriate for the festivities surround the door, and a second flagpole slants upward above a brass gong suspended on a post. *Courtesy* Sharlot Hall Museum.

ony. Subtle racial and cultural adjustment seems to have occurred without the awareness of either majority or minority (Figure 10). Such accommodation was made more dramatic by the continuing travail on the national level, which in 1892 promoted an extension of the Exclusion Act, and the bitter internecine warfare raging in the San Francisco Chinese ghetto which drove hundreds into the hinterlands. The degree to which resigned townsfolk of Prescott had adapted to historical reality is illustrated in an 1896 column in the *Courier*.

> Chinese, patient, sober, and business like, appear to make money in places where the white man fails. They have almost monopolized the cheap restaurant business and now the "sandwich wagon", that popular eating place that stands before "The Palace", has passed into the ownership of a cheerful son of Confucius.
>
> They occupy a similar position in [illegible] and also have well nigh absorbed the truck garden business as they squat on small fertile patches of ground that a white man would never think of looking at, and there with endless labor, they grow several crops a year and peddle vegetables to the local markets at all seasons. The Chinaman is the human burro. He can work 24 hours a day, keep fit on fruit can labels, and sleep comfortably in a bed with six other Chinamen piled on top of him.[121]

With the Chinese obviously in Prescott to stay, and some would admit to everyone's benefit, a few members of the host society felt that education in the English language and Christian doctrine might be an effective means for transforming alien and alienated Chinese into functioning participants in American life. Such a plan entailed considerable dedication on the part of all parties; communication and respect, whether spoken or implied, were prerequisite. Amends also needed to be made for past rebuffs and indifference. Through the influence of T. W. Otis, longtime befriender of the Chinese, a local church group of which he was an officer agreed to set up an instruction program in its tiny, white-frame place of worship. Expectedly, the texts were the Scriptures.

Although missionaries had been active in China from early in the nineteenth century, most Chinese came to America with no idea of Christianity. Their native religion was a polytheistic blend of Confucianism, Taoism, Buddhism, and animism toward which, in the eyes of devout American churchmen, they were surprisingly casual. Their ritual observances, such as the burning of "paper money"

---

121. *Prescott Morning Courier*, December 11, 1896.

whose smoke would reach the gods, focused on ancestor and spirit worship and were designed to ensure good health and worldly prosperity.[122] Regardless of how much of a religious impact the teachings of the Congregational Church might have made on its Chinese pupils, the following 1896 account of a program, written with unfamiliar studied graciousness, shows an atmosphere of mutual goodwill.

> The Congregational church was packed to its fullest capacity last evening with Prescott's ladies and gentlemen, to witness the entertainment given by the Chinese school of the church. The entertainment was gotten up entirely by the Chinese pupils, and the programs arranged by them. By way of introduction, T. W. Otis, superintendent of the school, made a statement giving a brief history of the school. It was started last March with ten pupils, and this number has increased during the year to thirty-five. The prime object of the school has been to teach the pupils the English language, but where it was agreeable to them, religious instruction has also been given to a voluntary choice of the pupils. The programme included the singing of two hymns in the Chinese language by the school, led by Rev. T. D. McLean, who has mastered enough of the Chinese language, to sing them. They were "There is a Happy Land" and "Stand up for Jesus", the tunes being familiar American ones.
>
> Lon Slung, a nineteen-year old boy, read a portion of a chapter from the New Testament in English and then read the same in Chinese, giving some of his views of it in Chinese also. His reading was quite distinct and clear, and showed remarkable rapid progress in the language, considering the fact that he has been less than a year acquiring his knowledge of it.
>
> Charley Wan, a well known Chinaman, gave a reading and also told a Chinese story about Mon Gee Hing in English, according to his own translation. The latter was particularly interesting, as some of his translations were particularly modern, and was in English as it is spoken, rather than written. An illustration being that in describing Mon Gee Hing's anger he stated that "he got hot" and others of similar import.

122. Clayre 1984: 35.

The Chirography of Lon Slung and Charley Wan is particularly good, being far better than that of the average American.

Kim Sam received an encore from the audience for a selection played on a Chinese harp, an instrument of quite sweet tones, although the music was peculiarly Chinese.

Chen Chung, Lou Dick, and Quen Long Hing gave an orchestral selection on a Chinese fiddle, a banjo, and flute.

After the exercises were over a very elaborate lunch consisting of ice cream, cake, nuts, and oranges was served to all present.[123]

The 1900 census provides limited identification of the Chinese performers on this occasion. Charlie Jon Wann, aged forty, married, and literate in English, was classed as a restaurant worker. He claimed to have come to the United States twenty-seven years earlier. Lou (Low) Dick, a forty-five-year-old laborer, had been in America a comparable period of time. Both men rented sleeping space in Chinatown. The most prosperous of the group seemed to be Quen (Quong Long) Hing, thirty-one-year-old owner of living quarters on Whiskey Row and operator of a general store. An earlier article called him a trader of crockery and tea. He claimed fifteen years in the United States. The lack of any listing of Lou Slung, Kim Sam, or Chen Chung resulted from the fact that at the time of the census they either had migrated to another locality or had returned to China. Apparently, the class of 1896 also included Joe Ah Jew, restaurateur.[124]

Not all Euro-Americans shared in the new-found admiration for the struggling Chinese, nor did the Asians cease their interminable in-fighting. A murder of one of them made the paper.

Sam Wing, gardener, was found dead in the road a short distance north of Robert Stead's early last Saturday morning by Jesse Henderson. Acting Coroner John M. Jones and Sheriff J. M. Thompson repaired to the place and found the body laid across the road, and the dead man's horses and wagon a mile farther north, with the two dogs that always accompanied the team.

123. Churches folder, Archives, Sharlot Hall Museum.
124. Parker 1941.

An examination of the body revealed gunshot wounds in the back of the head and neck and tracks behind a bush at the side of the road showed where the assassin had lain in wait for his victim; other tracks indicated that as the wagon passed he had advanced within eight feet and fired two fatal shots.

That the murder was not perpetrated for the purpose of robbery was that the body had not been approached and a watch and $10 were found on the person of the dead man. The murderer, after circling the spot, had returned to the road and toward Globe to within a quarter of a mile north of the Buffalo smelter, where the trail was lost.[125]

On a more pleasant note were two newspaper paragraphs promising more hope of the rare positive responses of the Chinese to American thought or actions. One mentioned that the Chinese band, using cymbals, drum, and clarinet, played in Granite Street to celebrate the christening of Prescott's only Chinese baby.[126] No such infant was recorded on the next census rolls, but perhaps he or she left town as a potential Christian. In reference to the Spanish-American War of 1898–1899, in which some Chinese served as cooks, seamen, and medical aides alongside United States troops,[127] the other item read,

> The Chinese are floating an American flag over their Joss House in Prescott. It is said to be on account of an article which appeared in a Chinese paper recently concerning Admiral Dewey's treatment of Chinese at Manila.[128]

During June 1900, federal census takers fanned out through Prescott to count 3,559 residents. Among them were 229 Chinese men, 4 women, and 5 children. That doubling of the number of Chinese residents since the last available figures of 1880 was the result of constant internal migration as the overseas Chinese sought the best

125. *Prescott Morning Courier*, December 13, 1896.
126. Unknown newspaper, February 27, 1898. Archives, Sharlot Hall Museum.
127. Strobridge 1984: 13–15. One Chinese buried in the G.A.R. plot of the Tucson Evergreen Cemetery, along with men who had come to Arizona with the California Volunteers, was a steward aboard the USS *Concord* during the battle of Manila Bay and was awarded a medal made from a captured Spanish cannon. He went on to serve in the U.S. Navy for twelve years and retired with a federal pension. *Arizona Daily Star*, Rodeo Edition, February 22, 1935.
128. *Arizona Republican*, May 21, 1898.

places for their peace and profit. The instability of this population is evident in the fact that few names can be traced through consecutive censuses.

Three of the Prescott Chinese men now had wives living with them. E. Foo Chung, laundryman, and his wife, E. Cum Ah, rented quarters, which they shared with five roomers. Merchant Kee Fow, with wife, nine-year-old son, and five-year-old daughter, also rented a dwelling large enough for three roomers. Cook Kee On owned a building at 132 South Granite Street, where he lived with his twenty-two-year-old wife, Jon Chut, and their ten-year-old daughter. At the tender age of twelve Jon Chut, a native of California, had given birth in Arizona to daughter Minnie. The fourth female, Gum Yow, was the last of the Chinese prostitutes to work in Prescott. One of the lost generation of Chinese girls, she stated she had been brought to the United States in 1869, when she was just four years old.

Data from the census revealed changes among the Prescott Chinese since the 1880 tabulation. The average age of these sojourners had risen to forty-two-plus years. This aging must be attributed to restricted immigration, but interestingly, almost a quarter of the immigrants indicated they had reached America after the 1882 ban. Since few were of the exempted group, why they would have admitted to such illegal entry is puzzling. Seventy-two others had been resident for twenty-five or more years. One old laundryman, who had arrived when a child of seven, said he had lived in America for forty-one years. In all that time, he had never learned to read or write English. Except for earning his income, he had lived his life almost as much within his own ethnic congregation as if he had never left China.

There were also more encouraging, albeit faint, signs of some future assimilation. A second generation of Chinese in diaspora had appeared. This reflected a similar phenomenon elsewhere, with approximately ten percent of the overseas Chinese in America at 1900 having been born there.[129] Locally, fifteen adults had been born in California, two in Oregon, and two youngsters in Arizona. Because of their places of birth, all were American citizens. Whether they exercised that privilege is undetermined. As far as China was concerned, they were Chinese citizens regardless of natal location.

129. Lee 1960: 39.

Approximately a fourth of the Chinese community was literate in English, with reading, writing, and speech skills of varying magnitude.

The range of occupations had expanded slightly, but it still had an overwhelming emphasis in 1900 on various facets of food services to keep Whiskey Row and its derivative businesses functioning. Laundry service remained a battleground, as the following advertisement shows.

> Do the Chinese support the schools: Nit! Do the chinks spend their money where they make it? Nein! Are they a credit to the country or an honor to the town? Nixey! Then why not send your clothes to a white institution? Hey? The Prescott Steam Laundry invites your patronage. D. M. Clark, Proprietor.[130]

There were no Chinese professionals in Prescott, although a fleeting reference to a doctor, who actually may have been an herbalist, had appeared in one paper ten years earlier.[131] In any event, doctors in China were held in low esteem.[132] The number of shopkeepers had increased from two to ten, but this was to keep pace with the demands of a larger ethnic market and to get around Exclusion Act restrictions against laborers. Their dealings with Euro-American consumers, and therefore possible integration into the broader society, likely were minimal.

Eight Chinese had accumulated enough resources to own their homes. Real estate was doubtless cheaper in Prescott than in west-coast cities, but such ownership does confirm that the Chinese acquisition of land was not restricted locally, as it was elsewhere. Thirty-six other Chinese served as heads of rented quarters, where groups of varying sizes shared meager accommodations. Several blocks of Granite Street continued to be Chinatown as far as structures were concerned, but many more Chinese lived elsewhere within the central business district. Laundries had dispersed, perhaps on guild orders, most likely so as to be closer to customers in the rooming houses that catered to single miners and railroad hands. By far the densest concentration of Chinese lodging was on Whiskey Row itself. The census shows that 119 persons lived over or

---

130. *Howler*, June 21, 1900.
131. *Prescott Morning Courier*, September 24, 1890.
132. Davis 1971: 29.

at the rear of this complex of bars and restaurants, which on contemporary maps are indicated only as Euro-American businesses. Therefore, Chinese residences do not appear there on Map 3. Merchants Quong Hing, E. Ah Wom, and Yee Kim owned houses at 156, 158, and 170 South Montezuma Street, respectively. Some Chinese occupied tenements opening onto the alley that ran through the block immediately west of the plaza. There were no Chinese at Whipple Barracks, owing to the fort's deactivation since 1898, when its troops left for Cuba and the Philippines to fight the Spanish-American War.[133] Four gardeners resided and farmed on lower Granite Creek near Point of Rocks. Two men called themselves peddlers of vegetables.

The composition of ethnic minorities in Prescott represented another change since 1880. As the Chinese had become the most important subgroup, the number of persons with Hispanic surnames had dropped to sixty-nine, of which twenty-one were children. Work by Hispanic men on the Santa Fe, Prescott, and Phoenix Railroad, which now connected the formerly isolated Arizona highlands to towns north and south, had replaced most wagon freighting. Other areas where they found work were manual labor and mining. One Hispanic woman was a housekeeper, one a seamstress, and two washed clothes on south Granite Street. The Hispanics were outnumbered by seventy-three blacks, five of whom were children. The black men were employed as barbers, porters, cooks, janitor, musician, bootblack, servants, and laborers. The women were cooks, waitress, housekeeper, and servant. Sixteen adult Japanese represented a racial entity new to the community. It was this group that competed most directly with the Chinese for jobs. Japanese men were cooks, restaurant managers, waiters, servants, and laborers. One Japanese woman was a prostitute, and two were laundresses.

Living conditions within the city block of which Whiskey Row was the eastern face must have been grim. These barest of facilities were notorious for extreme overcrowding, total lack of privacy, draftiness, rats, all-night noise, and the acrid odors of food preparation, stale beer, cigar smoke, and unwashed human bodies which wafted from the revelry department out front. On June 21, 1900, the *Howler* pleaded that the "alley between Granite and Montezuma

133. Yoder 1951: 50.

streets be cleaned up as the stench arising therefrom is terrible." It was, but in an unexpectedly devastating way.

On the evening of July 14 a drunken miner in town for a fling left a candle burning in his boardinghouse room while he went out for one more round. Shortly, the frame walls of the entire structure on the southwestern corner of Goodwin and Montezuma streets were ablaze. A summer wind fanned the flames northward. It was during the hot spell before the usual summer thunderstorms, so the creek and the town's reservoirs were dry, and the wells at each corner of the plaza were out of commission. The fire fiercely raged on, even though squads of frantic men tried to halt it by blasting buildings in its path. By morning, most of the central sector of Prescott had burned down. The entire block from the line of pleasure parlors on south Montezuma Street westward to the brothel cribs on south Granite Street was a smoldering mass of ashes and debris. The offensive alley in between had been cauterized. Amazingly, there had been no loss of life. Moreover, there had been sufficient time for shopkeepers and saloon patrons to drag merchandise and furnishings into the open plaza. With barrels of whiskey, an elaborate wooden bar, and a piano, the party continued.

Within several days the newspapers had set up temporary shop in spared parts of town and began recounting the damages. Grocery, dry-goods, and hardware stores, meat markets, the Western Union office, five hotels, twenty-five saloons, and the red-light district were gone. The loss was put at more than one million dollars, little of it covered by insurance. The point was made that it was the well-off businessmen who suffered, not the poor or destitute. In pages of newsprint about the disaster, there was not one word about the plight of more than a hundred Chinese who had lost their lodgings, as well as places of employment, in the destroyed concentration of Whiskey Row buildings. Almost as an aside and with some wry sarcasm about Chinese diligence, the *Howler* did note,

> Chinatown was saved by the hard work of its heathen occupants. The chinks saved their alarm clocks if nothing else.[134]

What actually remained of Chinatown was a row of five flimsy shacks on the northwest corner of Granite and Goodwin streets and an isolated building farther up the block which served as stores and

134. *Howler*, July 16, 1900.

[Figure 11] The westward view from the courthouse roof shows a block of buildings, destroyed by fire on July 14, 1900, known on its eastern face as Whiskey Row and on its southwestern face as the Red Light District. The lodgings of 119 Chinese on that block went up in flames, along with many of the town's saloons, restaurants, hotels, stores, and sporting parlors. The second street from the photographer's position is Granite Street, with the five original buildings of Chinatown and the joss house flagpole still intact. The trees behind border Granite Creek and the gable-roofed buildings on its western bank (still extant) which housed the tenth and possibly the eleventh Arizona territorial legislatures. *Courtesy* Sharlot Hall Museum.

living quarters (Figure 11). As the fire ate away their tenements and a store on the east side of Granite Street, the Chinese hurriedly soaked blankets and mattresses, draped them as best they could over the fronts of the west-side buildings, and kept the dirt street in front wet with a bucket brigade. The wind obliged by staying its northerly course. The two Chinese laundries along north Granite Street, one on Gurley Street, and a third on north Cortez Street went up in smoke.

Presumably, those who had bedded down behind Whiskey Row were able to cart at least some of their few possessions away to safety. They surely crowded in with their kinsmen lucky enough to have escaped the destruction or camped out in the hills until new quarters could be arranged. Within a year, the original group of

Chinatown buildings had been expanded back toward Granite Creek and northward along the west side of south Granite Street (Map 4). Since most of the buildings were rented from Euro-American landlords, it is probable that, through one of their associations, the Chinese pooled monies to pay for these additions. Their homeless had been cared for, and not a single Chinese individual had asked for a loan from the fund established to aid victims of the Great Prescott Fire of 1900.

That fire marked a turning point in the history of the local Chinese colony. Some Asian cooks quickly set up temporary soup kitchens in the middle of Montezuma Street, where they dispensed hot meals for thirty-five cents,[135] but others grew discouraged at the loss of steady income while Euro-Americans rebuilt their places of business. Many must have moved on to greener pastures. That may have been Tucson or Phoenix in Arizona, where other Chinese were settling. Most likely it was Los Angeles or San Francisco; the ties of the Chinese in north-central Arizona always had been to the Pacific coast. Some decided that the sojourn of many dreams and few realizations was over. They went home.

All over the Rocky Mountain states a slow Chinese retreat from small towns or rural situations into urban slums already was occurring. Metropolitan Chinatowns offered the displaced Chinese reassurance, protection, job opportunities, and, if necessary, financial assistance. Since the Asians survived only on a tenuous interrelationship with the majority Euro-American community, their migrations of the 1890–1910 era in large part were precipitated by Euro-American economic advance or reverse.[136] In the case of Prescott, the fire, which occurred at the beginning of this period of significant demographic change was the event that capped the expansion of the Chinese and initiated a perceptible decline in their numbers.

After four decades in Prescott, no social stratification had occurred within the Chinese colony because there had been no labor market for skilled workers or educated professionals. The lower-class individuals who did come succeeded only in obtaining the least lucrative and least status-enhancing jobs because, although no formal organized labor front stood against them, a subtle form of a

135. Allen 1941.
136. Lee 1949: 422–32; 1960: 36.

labor caste system kept them outside the mainstream. Contributing to this situation were a complex mix of racial and cultural attitudes of both dominant and minority societies, fear on the part of Euro-Americans of economic competition, and the impossibility of Chinese familial living, which conceivably would have provided motivation for more rapid Americanization.

THE CHINESE ARE LEAVING

The departure of the Prescott Chinese did not occur overnight. It spread over more than three decades, almost the same amount of time it had taken for them to reach their numerical peak. During those years local perception of them mellowed as official governmental policy hardened.

One of those who made the decision to return to China was Charlie Jan Wann, former pupil of the Congregational Church school and manager of a restaurant owned by banker M. B. Hazeltine. Once back home in 1902, with his command of English, Christian conversion, business skills, and sideline witnessing of modern medical, sanitation, and technological practices, he shed his American alias. As Jan Con Sang, he became one of the wealthiest merchants in cosmopolitan Hong Kong (Figure 12). Before his death during the World War II Japanese occupation, he had acquired a string of retail stores called the Sincere Company, a fleet of river boats, a railroad, interest in the National Commercial and Savings Bank of Hong Kong, and had founded a hospital and middle school run by the church. His sons were businessmen and a doctor.[137] Jan Con Sang's hard life as a sojourner gave him no reason to forsake his cultural roots in order to become superficially Americanized. Nonetheless, there is no doubt that his nearly thirty years abroad, in addition to his intelligence and motivation, provided some of the keys to his ultimate success. Perhaps for both countries concerned, his was the best possible kind of cultural enrichment.

Meanwhile, the rough-hewn wooden architecture of Prescott had been replaced by blocks of substantial, fireproof (it was hoped),

---

137. Parker 1941; Archives, Sharlot Hall Museum.

[Figure 12] On the occasion of his seventieth birthday, patriarch Jan Con Sang sits for a family portrait at his home in China. As Charlie Jan Wann, he had lived in the Prescott Chinatown for nearly thirty years, where he worked his way into the position of manager of a local restaurant. After the 1900 town fire, he returned to Hong Kong to put his managerial skills to work acquiring a fortune and power. The photograph confirms that, despite his lengthy sojourn in America and later residency in a British Crown Colony, Jan Con Sang had rejected outward signs of Westernization for himself, his wife, and their offspring. *Courtesy* Sharlot Hall Museum.

brick buildings of mixed styles. On Whiskey Row many Euro-American owners no longer chose to include even minimal housing for employees. With quartz mines in the back country flourishing and ranching beginning to show signs of profitability, the town's population gradually increased and turned conservative. Wives arrived to set up households and take over the domestic chores of washing and cooking. It was the Chinese who now were being threatened with competition. Additionally, the laundrymen were slapped with a new tax, but they were docile victims no longer, as the case of Tom Kee illustrates.

> Because he told Deputy Assessor E. W. Stephens to go to a warmer place than Yuma and refused to give the names of employees of his wash house so that school tax could be collected from them and in addition refused to contribute his

annual mite toward the cost of maintaining the public schools of the territory, Tom Kee, Chinese, paid a fine of $20 in the justice court yesterday in lieu of spending twenty days in the county jail. [Tom Kee's laundry was at 114 South Granite Street.]

When arraigned in court the rebellious Chink did not deny the charges preferred. He relented, however, when he saw the bars of the county bastile open to receive him with the prospect of being appointed an assistant to the plaza gardener in improving the promenades around the court house. He said he no likee the law that compels a hard-working washee man to pay $2.50 a year for the privilege of starching white shirts in addition to his other taxes. His furtive glances at Deputy Stephens and the court indicated that he was impressed that they were not gentlemen, although he wisely reserved giving expression to his opinions. He claimed that one of his Celestial assistants was an attache of the Quail restaurant, and that he ought not to be compelled to pay his poll tax. Inquiry at the restaurant showed Kee to be a trifler with the truth.

In addition to paying the fine of $20 he was compelled to fork over $2.50 each for every Celestial found in his wickiup before he was released.[138]

As if these setbacks were not trouble enough, in 1907 gambling became illegal in the Arizona Territory,[139] there was talk of suppressing prostitution because of the presence of more proper ladies, and the local police were taking dimmer views of opium smoking. On top of all that, immigration officers were making life miserable.

The ineffectual efforts after 1882 to stop Chinese laborers from entering the United States had been likened to stepping on ants. Some were eliminated, but the swarm relentlessly kept on coming. For all the masses that were turned away, thousands of others slipped in by means of multitudinous clandestine plans carried out by Chinese already resident, particularly criminal elements in tongs, and by American and Mexican cohorts eager to make fast profits. Increased government forces were hard put to distinguish between those who sneaked in and those who had arrived legally during the

138. *Arizona Journal Miner*, March 16, 1909.
139. Bret Harte 1980: 89.

previous thirty years. The latter had been promised the right to reenter under certain conditions after a return visit to China. Moreover, those who had been born in the United States were exempt from the Exclusion Act. Arizona's long, unguarded southern border proved a point of relatively painless unauthorized entrance, as some officials paid only token attention to the Exclusion Act. The Third Judicial District docket book of Prescott reveals that all cases booked prior to 1891 against Chinese unlawfully in the country were dismissed with protests of overloaded court calendars.[140] A survey of extant records shows that the district and superior bodies seemingly were more interested in prosecuting cases of polygamy among the Mormons, of adultery and fornication among the Hispanics, and of the sale of liquor to the Native Americans by everyone.

Enforcement of the law stepped up after 1892, when every Chinese man, woman, and child of nonexempt status was required to register and to carry identifying documentation that included an individual photograph and physical description. The Six Companies mistakenly believed the act to be unconstitutional and advised the Chinese not to register as aliens. Noncompliance with the law put thousands in jeopardy and exacerbated an already explosive situation. The highbinders put a price on the head of the Six Companies' leaders in the knowledge that tong members were particularly vulnerable as undesirables.[141] That, in turn, brought on internal Chinese warfare.[142] However, the requisite photographs were an aid to agents, who confessed that to them "all Chinese looked alike." Documentation in itself, nevertheless, compounded the problem, since there was an immediate ubiquity of forged, stolen, or purchased certificates of residence called *chock chee*. Frustrated but determined, American agents manfully tried to carry out their mandates, as a newspaper clip from the *Arizona Republican* confirms.

> Five Chinamen were brought from Prescott on Saturday night's train under sentence of deportation to the land of their fathers.[143]

---

140. Hall 1980.
141. Dillon 1962: 17.
142. *San Francisco Chronicle*, May 17, 1893.
143. *Arizona Republican*, August 7, 1899.

The *Arizona Republican* item may have referred to Yee Tung (alias Tony), Wong Tong Sung, Lee Fong, Leong Jim, Gin Fon Geou, and Gate (alias Ah Geh), all of whom were arrested in Prescott in 1899 to be shipped back to the Empire of China from San Francisco on the steamship *Gaelic.* Five of the men offered no defense; one claimed to have lost his certificate of residence.[144]

Fearful of being arrested and having to bear the expense of an appeal trial, as well as its mortification, some Chinese with legitimate claims to residency in the United States sought legal clarification of their status. One such person was Ah Poy, a youth of eighteen years, who said he had been born in San Francisco. He was in Prescott in 1897 living with Quong Yuen, a Chinese merchant who once had worked for Ah Poy's father. The court accepted Ah Poy's California birth and provided him with papers to that effect.

Tuck Chung, petitioning the court in 1897, desired papers to show that he was a bonafide merchant. He stated that for three years he had worked and been a partner in the store of Quong Hing, "just China grocery store, and something to sell for the Chinaman," as he said. Quong Hing and William Wilkerson, a Euro-American resident of Prescott for twenty-seven years, testified on his behalf.

A similar case was that of Yee Sing. Prior to coming to Prescott, he had kept a store of Chinese and Japanese goods in Kingston, New Mexico Territory. He did not apply for a certificate of residence when the 1892 revision of the Exclusion Act was enacted because, as a merchant, he was not compelled to do so. Later he sold his store, went to China, and subsequently was permitted reentry. But just to protect himself against any future arrest and possible deportation, he sought identifying papers. Harriet H. Hoes, a resident of Prescott in 1897 who earlier had lived in Kingston, vouched for him (Figure 13).

Tom Wey Lung was picked up by officers and, having no certificate of residence, was ordered deported in 1899. He appealed, with the aid of attorney Eugene Brady O'Neill, claiming merchant status in San Francisco. Each such person appealing deportation orders had to post bond through two individuals serving as sureties. In Tom Wey Lung's case, the sureties were Prescott merchants Quong

---

144. Chinese Exclusion Case Files, 1897–1911, Third and Fourth Judicial District, Arizona Territory, National Archives, Los Angeles Branch.

[Figure 13] Yee Sing was a shopkeeper who moved to Prescott from Kingston, New Mexico Territory, in the late 1890s. To protect himself from possible deportation he secured legal papers declaring him to be a long-time resident of the United States and a bonafide merchant. An American acquaintance living in Prescott, Marriet H. Hoes, vouched from him. *Courtesy* National Archives, Los Angeles Branch.

Hing and Quong Yuen. They had to swear "that he [Tom Wey Lung] is a resident freeholder in the county of Yavapai, Territory of Arizona, and is worth the sum of Two Hundred and Fifty Dollars over and above his just debt and liabilities exclusive of property exempt from execution." The court ruled in Tom Wey Lung's favor.

Those Chinese returning from home leave who were detained at disembarkation ports frequently had to rely on their Euro-American, as well as Chinese, colleagues to vouch for them and their mandatory merchant status. One such instance involved Yee Chung, a Granite Street businessman in partnership with relative Sam Chung and Woo and Yung Sing. According to 1900 census information, he had come to the United States in 1879 but apparently had not bothered to obtain a certificate of residence. Upon arriving in San Francisco, he was required to prove his stated occupation. Testimony taken from Guilford Hathaway, Prescott pioneer then engaged in freighting, indicated that the house and lot occupied by the present store had been transferred in 1891 from Fong Ben to Sun Quong Wo, who sold it four years later to Quong

Yen, from whom it passed to Yee Chung's company. Other witnesses subpoenaed were T. W. Otis, attorney John Howard, Gee Mun, and C. Woo, a Prescott laundryman for ten years who had served such local dignitaries as judges Hawkins and Andrews and businessmen Morrison, Johnston, and Burmister. The hearings were sufficiently satisfactory to permit Yee Chung to return to Prescott.

Caught in the confused web of exclusionary laws was another pair of the town's Chinese, whom some compassionate Euro-American neighbors helped reenter.

> Fong Murphy and Hee Long, both well-known Chinese residents of Prescott, are in trouble in San Francisco. They have been on a visit to the flowery kingdom, and on their return trip were refused permission to land at San Francisco. Murphy is a member of the Kwong Hing mercantile company here as well as the most popular Chinese caterer that lived here. Hee Long is also a restaurant man. A petition for permission for them to land will be forwarded to San Francisco.[145]

Back in town by the time of the 1900 census tabulation, Hee Long, who claimed to have been in the United States since 1871, said he lived at 158 South Montezuma Street. His companion, Fong Murphy, then fifty-five years old and a resident in the United States since 1874, roomed down the block at number 164. After all their legal difficulties, they had returned to Prescott just in time to be burned out in the great July fire. It must have posed a critical decision for Hee Long; he was gone by the next census. Undaunted, the personable Fong Murphy continued stirring his cookpots in Prescott until July 5, 1912, when he was placed to final rest in the Citizens Cemetery.[146]

Regional deportation activity quieted for the next few years, although in 1902 Chinese exclusion was made permanent. Only one man, Jong Shan Chow, was apprehended that year.[147] In 1903 Lee Yuen, Ben Yam, and Ka Suey, served with arrest warrants on the streets of Prescott, soon found themselves on their way back to China. Merchants Quong Hing and Quong Yuen again were sureties for one of these unfortunates; gardeners Joe Bing and Joe Lee

---

145. *Arizona Journal Miner*, quoted in *Arizona Republican*, June 23, 1899.

146. Mortuary records, Archives, Sharlot Hall Museum.

147. Chinese Exclusion Case Files, 1897–1911, Third and Fourth Judicial District District, Arizona Territory, National Archives, Los Angeles Branch.

filled a similar role for another. Gin Ling Chong had the pleasure of having his American birth verified. The case of Quong Yick, for whom Prescottonians G. W. Middleton and C. P. Hicks were sureties, was dismissed. The year 1904 saw three more Chinese deportation cases before the court. Yee Wing, who made the mistake of trying to bribe Inspector Connel with one hundred dollars, was deported.[148] Ham Wo Chung, with the team of Quong Hing and Quong Yuen as sureties, was exonerated. After receipt of a deposition from a former chief justice of the Colorado Supreme Court, Yee Lee also was freed.

The deportation battles never stopped, but the proverbially clever Chinese were quick to try to turn the disaster of the 1906 San Francisco earthquake and fire to their advantage. Inasmuch as all the vital birth and immigration records of the western region were lost in that event, it was soon learned by the hopeful immigrants that United States agents could not easily disprove their claims of citizenship based on birth in California. One resigned official estimated that every Chinese woman known to have been in the state prior to the earthquake must have given birth to one hundred fifty sons.[149] Although cross-examination was intense, demanding intimate knowledge of the alleged birthplace and all nearby nooks and crannies, generally there was nothing that could be done but accept what were suspected to be fraudulent claims of American birth. Another common Chinese defense, that certificates of residence were consumed by fires, was made with the confidence that harassed officers could not prove otherwise.

Taking up this plea was Hee Kau, apprehended in Prescott in 1907 and out on a five-hundred-dollar bond through the courtesy of two local Euro-Americans. His was a typical story of sojourner peregrinations, always in quest of an illusive jackpot. Supposedly having been a merchant and then newspaper printer in Honolulu, Hee Kau moved on to San Francisco just prior to the city's destruction. Of course, his legal papers vanished as a result. From there, he went to Phoenix and finally to Prescott. In that upland village he had found employment for a few months as a dishwasher at the Quail Restaurant. Still restless, Hee Kau drifted east to the mining

148. *Phoenix Daily Enterprise*, January 18, 1904.
149. Perkins 1984: 223.

town of Humboldt and a job waiting tables at the Lee On Restaurant. That proved temporary, so he went a few miles farther down the road to Poland. There he worked as a waiter in the boarding-house of the Poland Mining Company. It was an aimless existence but one the court allowed him to continue.[150]

The Customs Bureau assembled a task force called Chinese Inspectors in order to strengthen efforts for ferreting out those who had no legitimate claims to be in the United States.[151] Prescott came under the jurisdiction of the office set up on the Santa Fe Railroad at Seligman. Local sojourners seemed to know through an effective grapevine when an inspector was headed south toward Prescott. Then the nervous but outwardly imperturbable cousins rallied round to testify to the honesty of their kinsman and to post bond, even though that man might have arrived in the country only a week or two earlier. The motivation was suddenly at hand to learn at least minimal English: inspectors were less suspicious of those who could answer a few questions in the tongue of the land. The Methodist Episcopal mission school built on south Granite Street to educate the Chinese therefore had little difficulty in getting a student body. All in all, the quest for illegal entrants became a cat-and-mouse game without equitable solution.

The widespread abuse of the American law by the Chinese subjected them to years of fear, suspicion, and blackmail within their own ranks when tongs preyed on men in the country with no or phony papers, demanded extortion payments, or took it upon themselves to punish informers. It was a vicious gangland struggle, which for a dozen years American police were unable to check owing to the closed nature of overseas Chinese enclaves, termed by Dillon the "conspiracy of silence."[152] Law-abiding Chinese were afraid to speak out in the face of threats from colleagues and ignorance of American legalities.

A poignant episode with tragic consequences for two local men rocked the Prescott Chinese. The newspaper account of it is revealing on a number of levels. First, there was the lengthy stay in China

---

150. Chinese Exclusion Case Files, 1897–1911, Third and Fourth Judicial District, Arizona Territory, National Archives, Los Angeles Branch.

151. Perkins 1984: 217–32.

152. Dillon 1962: 244.

of Yee Thoi Goung. Actually, his two-year visit was average. Being at home and living idly off his profits for that long of a period allowed a man to demonstrate how successful his sojourn had been and so inspire envy in others.[153] If single, he had time perhaps to find a wife, build a new home, and father a child, preferably a son. Second, the article points to the desperate need many felt to stay at work in the United States and the evil forces within all the Chinese communities which thrived on that desire. It also spotlights two highly characteristic Chinese attitudes: cultivated stoicism and a deeply felt need for preserving at least the outward appearance of dignity and acceptance.

> After three years of legal fighting in which many technicalities of the law were invoked, Yee Thoi Goung, Chinese who has been engaged in business in this city for the past twenty-seven years, left here last night in custody of Deputy United States Marshal A. E. Barton, to be deported, with thirty-five other Celestials, now at Tucson, to the Flowery Kingdom.
>
> Yee Thoi Goung obeyed the orders of the court with the stolid indifference peculiar to his race. It was evident from his conversations, however, that he has not abandoned the legal fight for permission to remain here, where he has been a leader of his race so long and where he has been prosperous in business. He stated last evening that he would refer his case to the Chinese consul at San Francisco, immediately upon his arrival in his native land.
>
> Yee Thoi Goung left here for China in 1902, going by way of San Francisco. He was armed with the necessary papers and registered regularly at the San Francisco port before his departure. On his return there in 1904, he was confronted with the accusation that he was not a merchant, but in reality the proprietor of a "hop joint" in this city. The charge was preferred by one of the Chinese Six Companies, which was at war at that time with the company of which Goung was a member. He was deported to China, but later returned here by way of Mexico. He came into the United States through Nogales,

153. Lee 1960: 83.

escaping arrest by the immigration officers, at the line, but being caught here later.

August 20, 1907, he was ordered deported by United States Commissioner Moore, much to the surprise of the leading Chinese residents of the town, many of whom became greatly excited over the sentence. Quong Hing, another Chinese merchant and an oldtime resident, was openly accused by members of the Chinese colony of giving information to the officers that led to the deportation sentence and, it is said, was sentenced to death by a local Chinese tong. A Chinese hatchetman, of San Francisco, was pressed into service, but before he could execute the death sentence, Quong Hing, feeling keenly the disgrace of the charge, repaired to the Citizens cemetery, a few evenings before the final time limit allowed him expired, and committed suicide by taking an overdose of opium. He was found the following morning, still alive, and removed to the hospital, where all efforts to revive him proved futile, his death following a few hours later.

Chinatown was much wrought up over what was considered the enforced suicide of Quong Hing and for several weeks the Chinese residents all went armed, expecting a Tong war to break out at any moment.[154]

Although the basic fact of deportation is confirmed by surviving legal records, many details of this affair differ or are more fully described in those documents. In papers filed before he made a trip to China in January 1899, Yee Thoi Goung claimed to be one of five related partners in the Quong Hing Company, located on Granite Street. Yee Chin was the manager, and Yee Thoi Goung was the bookkeeper. The other members of the company were Quong Hing, owner of the store and of a Whiskey Row building, Yee Chow, and Yee Ching Goung. Later described as occupying a nine-room frame building, that store must have been at the northwest corner of Granite and Goodwin streets, inasmuch as no other structure shown on a contemporary map was of that size. Yee Thoi Goung valued the stock of the business at four thousand dollars in real estate, Japanese and Chinese goods, and other personal proper-

154. *Prescott Journal Miner*, March 10, 1908.

ties. Three prominent Euro-American citizens of Prescott witnessed the departure papers, which also bore the signatures of J. M. Watts, court clerk, and John W. Dougherty, then mayor.

The following year a valuation of three thousand dollars was placed on the Quong Hing Company. Yee Thoi Goung had not returned from China, but his photograph was identified by M. B. Hazeltine and R. W. Burmister, both of whom recognized him as a local merchant.

In July 1902 Yee Thoi Goung returned from his home visit aboard the SS *Doric*, but word was received in Prescott that he was being held at San Francisco. There was doubt as to his merchant status. The newsman's suspicions of tong interference likely were correct. Someone had tipped off the American officials that Yee Thoi Goung actually should be considered an undesirable alien engaged in activities other than shopkeeping. Meantime, another document evaluating the store at five thousand dollars was signed by Hazeltine, president of the Arizona Bank; Jake Marks, wholesale liquor dealer; Burmister, merchant and current mayor; Morris Goldwater, merchant and member of the Commercial Trust Company; and the president of the Prescott National Bank. Who could ask for more respected references?

To determine the actual situation, Chinese Inspector George W. Webb made the trip from his headquarters at Tucson to Prescott. He found only an estimated one hundred dollars worth of dry goods and groceries and two hundred dollars worth of liquors in one room of the alleged store. The eight other rooms seemed to be for lodging and for smoking opium, where at the time of his surprise visit there were seven men lying on bunks in various states of opium intoxication. This was incriminating evidence indeed.

In a follow-up conversation with Hazeltine, Webb further learned that Yee Thoi Goung was known to have been a heavy gambler and flasher of cash. George Gates, deputy city marshal of Prescott, chimed in to note that gambling in the form of "Chinese lottery" and "tan" had gone on at the establishment for the past eight years. All was legal, however, because necessary licenses had been obtained from the city from 1897 through July 1902. At that point, just when Yee Thoi Goung was trying to get beyond the detention center at San Francisco, such activity abruptly ceased. Similar testimony about gambling was given by the under-sheriff, the city marshal, and the city tax collector.

The next month, in a second visit to the store, Inspector Webb found that the store stocks had been dramatically increased. Dry goods, groceries, and Chinese drugs, valued at twenty-five hundred dollars, and liquors valued at three hundred dollars were then on the shelves, giving the appearance of a thriving outlet for Chinese household needs.

The skeptical inspector reported to his boss, the customs collector at Nogales, that in addition to the evidence of gambling and opium sale and use, he was not impressed by the words of Hazeltine, who admitted he had been in the store only once or twice, or of Marks, who had business dealings through the sale of spirits to the company. To Webb, the precipitous addition to the inventory and the sudden halt of gambling were highly suspicious attempts to legitimize Yee Thoi Goung's status. Moreover, J. P. Storm, county treasurer, reduced the company assets from $1,400 in 1897 to $1,050 in 1901. This was not sufficient investment for each of the five partners to meet the legal standards for a Chinese merchant in good standing. The evidence against the sojourner seemed overwhelming.

On October 24, 1902, Yee Thoi Goung was returned to China on the SS *Coptic*.

When he voluntarily went home in 1899, Yee Thoi Goung likely was treated with deference owing to the money and gifts he brought and his doubtless exaggerated tales of exploits and success in America. To return as a penniless reject was quite another matter. Without funds or ready employment and long out of tune with daily family routine, he must have been a sorrowful misfit. Quite probably he and similar outcasts spent their time plotting new assaults on the United States.

Five years later Yee Thoi Goung, recorded then as Yee Phoi Going, again crossed the Pacific, this time docking in Guaymas, Mexico, where Chinese still were accepted. He made his way to the United States border and within a month was arrested in Tucson by Inspector Webb, whose bloodhound instincts apparently included a photographic memory. As was his privilege, Yee Thoi Goung appealed and was released under an unusually high bond of seven hundred fifty dollars. He lost his battle, however. On March 30, 1908, the United States marshal escorted him aboard the SS *China*, never to return to Prescott (Figure 14). By that time the man

[Figure 14] Yee Thoi Goung was one of five partners in a Granite Street business during the late 1890s and the first decade of the twentieth century. His Certificate of Residence, issued in Santa Fe in 1894, describes him as both a laborer and shop-keeper. In 1902 Yee Thoi Goung was detained in San Francisco upon his return from China because of allegations that his primary business in Prescott was a gambling and opium-smoking parlor. He is shown here against a document signed by several prominent Anglo citizens of Prescott verifying his merchant status. Federal officers however felt that the suspicions of undesirable activities were well founded and ordered that Yee Thoi Goung be deported. Meanwhile back in Prescott, one of his partners was accused of informing on him and committed suicide in a local cemetery in shame. Five years later Yee Thoi Goung slipped back into Arizona from Mexico. He was apprehended in Tucson, and deported for a second time in 1908. *Courtesy* National Archives, Los Angeles Branch.

alleged to have turned him in, the owner of the company of which he was a one-time partner, was dead by his own hand.[155]

Combined threats of deportation, subversion, and retribution seem to have kept the Prescott Chinese agitated. Still, much of what we read today may have been press sensationalism.

> That another Tong War, with greater ramifications than the last one which threw the local Chinatown into a state of panic, and which was only prevented from assuming most serious proportions by the opportune suicide of a prominent Chinese leader, who had been marked for death by imported hatchet-men, is imminent, is the belief of Wa Hing, whose laundry located between the city hall and the Fashion livery stable [Wo Hing laundry was at 129 South Granite Street in the 1900 census] was discovered on fire last night, at 8:35 o'clock.
>
> Investigation revealed indubitable evidence that the fire was of incendiary origin, and Wa Hing's assistant, who was in the laundry at the time, and succeeded in extinguishing the flames before any serious damage was done the building, while maintaining the secretive silence characteristic of the oriental race, made it plain, in the stress of excitement following the fire, that he was convinced that someone with a grievance against Wa Hing had fired the soiled-linen establishment.
>
> Immediately after it became known that some one had set fire to the place there was a quick gathering of Wa Hing's Chinese friends, who, in excited converse, discussed the probable identity of the incendiary, and made a second examination of the premises, discovering that the fire had been kindled at a rear door to the laundry which was covered with canvas. The flames were traveling rapidly toward the roof when extinguished.
>
> It is known that an official connected with the Chinese immigration service arrived here yesterday from Tucson, and while it could not be ascertained whether or not he had held a conference with Wa Hing, or any of the latter's employees, it was intimated by a prominent member of the Chinese colony last evening that possibly someone, fearing Wa Hing might

155. U. S. Register of Actions, Chinese Exclusion Docket Book, Fourth Judicial District, Arizona Territory, Box 1, National Archives, Los Angeles Branch.

give information to the immigration official concerning some of the Chinamen here who may not be provided with the necessary Chock Gee, had fired the laundry as a gentle warning to Wa Hing to maintain discreet silence if questioned. Wa Hing himself denies that he knows anything concerning any Chinamen who may be in the country illegally, and blandly insists that he hasn't an enemy in all the wide world.

Nevertheless, Chinatown is all agog over the possibility of a Tong outbreak and the importation of the hatchetmen who were robbed of the intended victim on their last visit here by his suicide.[156]

Sometimes investigations into Chinese backgrounds took years to resolve, owing to inconsistency in defendant and witness statements and to the difficulties of tracking down persons among the extremely mobile migrant community who could substantiate testimony. Mock Wing, born in San Francisco in the Chinese year of Kwang Suey 24, spent two years trying to clear himself (Figure 15).[157] As an infant, he had been taken back to the Orient, where he had remained for two decades. During his young manhood in China, he had married, fathered several children, and worked as a farm hand. Then, hoping to improve his lot, he had returned to America and been admitted. Mock Wing had washed dishes in restaurants in San Francisco and Flagstaff and in the boardinghouse of the United Verde and Pacific Railroad in order to support himself. Ultimately, he came to Prescott, where for five years he worked for the Santa Fe, Prescott, and Phoenix Railroad. A round trip to China following that interval landed him in the arms of the law, since he carried no identification. Understandably, over the years Mock Wing had been such a transient among scores of other transients that he could not readily find persons who could corroborate his birth, family, or whereabouts at any given time. Patience was finally rewarded, however, when two San Francisco associates came

---

156. *Arizona Journal Miner*, February 19, 1908.

157. The Chinese calendar, based on twelve months of twenty-nine or thirty days, with an extra month added every thirty months, began in 2697 B.C. It was a system of sixty-year cycles, Kwang Suey being the one in progress during the period of the territorial sojourners. The Gregorian calendar was adopted in 1912 with the establishment of the Chinese Republic.

[Figure 15] Mock Wing, detained in Prescott in 1909 without a Certificate of Residence, claimed to have had a legal document substantiating his birth in San Francisco. Supposedly, the paper had been burned during a restaurant fire in Williams. After two years of searching for witnesses to corroborate his story, the testimonies of Woo Kee Wing and Woo Chung Hin were taken by deposition, and the fact of Mock Wing's citizenship through native birth was accepted. The case against him was dropped upon payment of court costs. *Courtesy* National Archives, Los Angeles Branch.

forward to swear to his veracity. In 1911 the case against Mock Wing was vacated on payment of costs.[158]

158. Chinese Exclusion Case Files, 1897–1911, Third and Fourth Judicial District, Arizona Territory, National Archives, Los Angeles Branch.

During the period Mock Wing was under investigation, at least three other Prescott Chinese were escorted from the country. They were Gee Wing, Wong Deen (alias Yeon Long), and Wee Guon Foo. They brought the total number of local deportations during the last dozen years of the territorial era to eighteen, with ten other men being cleared by reason of citizenship or occupation. Steadily, it seemed, the ranks were being depleted.

Nevertheless, fear of American rejection or punishment was not as troublesome to the Chinese as worry over merciless retribution by other countrymen for a variety of supposed offenses. The following item spotlights the prevailing undercurrent of fear.

> Rapid headway is being made in a Chinese Tong war in this city, and every day makes the glow of the horizon tinge with a crimson hue.
>
> Intimations are rife in the Chinese quarter that the "hatchetman", who swings mysteriously after the Chink fashion, is en route, and all know what that means. Lin Fee, charged with forgery and a member of one tong, was yesterday released on bonds placed at $1000 by Judge McLane, and is again among his clansmen stoutly maintaining that his arrest is one of persecution, adding that he and his friends will go to the limit to disprove the charges. One prominent Chinaman of the city yesterday said that it looks "velly bad", which is significant that something in the line of a vendetta is in prospect in the Chinatown of Prescott.[159]

Like most rumors, they were nothing more. According to Dillon, the 1906 San Francisco earthquake and fire that leveled the Chinatown there also brought an end to the tong battles.[160] However, with or without an open tong war, there seldom was peace in Prescott's Chinese quarter. The rebellious Tom Kee, then working in what must have been one of the first so-called noodle joints on south Granite Street, got into a fight with four soldiers on leave, who pushed him against a hot stove, causing severe burns.[161] Another bloody altercation occurred at a second eatery on the corner

159. *Arizona Journal Miner*, December 9, 1909.
160. Dillon 1962: 50.
161. *Arizona Journal Miner*, September 10, 1908.

of Granite and Goodwin streets between a group of blacks and what the paper called "most of Chinatown." There were serious injuries on both sides.[162] Quong Ning was apprehended in Jerome after passing a bad check for two hundred dollars in Prescott.[163] Kim Sam, Granite Street merchant, stood trial for burning down the adjoining eatery operated by Lee Lin. Five months later the case was dismissed when two tong factions gave contradictory testimony and the principal witnesses left the country.[164] A raid in March 1911 netted Chin Mark Sam, Yee Ing, and Ung Chuck, who were charged with smuggling opium prepared for smoking from Mexico. The same year Leo Hung was sentenced to ninety days and fined one hundred dollars for providing an Indian one gill (a half pint) of liquor. Unable to pay the fine, Leo Hung served an additional month in jail.[165]

In spite of this pattern of turbulence, some Prescottonians had relaxed their attitudes toward their Chinese neighbors. Others still exhibited little understanding. Nothing reveals both points of view more clearly than a brief account of an incident that took place during a 1908 Chinese New Year celebration.

> As a party of Americans entered the Joss house last night one of the women in the party stepped up to the high dignitary of the local Chinese and asked: "Me wantee see Chink-a-Chink smokum hop, John. Alle samee you slavvee?" The grave Oriental maintained an unruffled calm and dignified silence, but when her request was repeated, only in a still more outlandish jargon similar to the above, he lost patience.
>
> "Madam, you are an American. Why on earth don't you speak intelligent English?"
>
> It is needless to add that she hastily withdrew from his presence.[166]

During the almost forty years the Chinese had lived in the Prescott vicinity, there had been a number of deaths among them,

162. *Arizona Journal Miner*, October 27, 1909.
163. *Arizona Journal Miner*, May 9, 1909.
164. *Arizona Journal Miner*, July 7, July 10, November 19, 1909.
165. Criminal Case Files, 1891–1911, Third and Fourth Judicial District, Arizona Territory, National Archives, Los Angeles Branch.
166. *Arizona Journal Miner*, February 8, 1908.

including several murders at at least two suicides in addition to that of Quong Hing. In 1900 Quai Chung, a single barber, had killed himself by unknown methods.[167] The third suicide occurred not in response to undue outside pressures but rather because of the culturally implanted face-saving syndrome.

> There was only one untoward incident to mar the celebration of the new year. This was the death of Charles Shut, who was found dead in Miller's Lane, just as the rising sun greeted the first day of the Chinese new year. It is said that Shut, unable to comply with Chinese tradition, which provides that all obligations must be paid off before the entrance of the new year, drank himself to death to avoid the disgrace of being in debt on New Year's day. Shut's funeral, it was noticed, was not attended with the usual pomp and ceremony pertaining to the burial of a Chinaman.[168]

Charles Shut was buried in Citizens Cemetery by the Ruffner Mortuary, a local territorial institution.[169]

Chinese funerals, held at the temple and in front of it on Granite Street, always had drawn a few curious Euro-American onlookers, whom the mourners welcomed with quiet forbearance (Figure 16). After the turn of the century, which brought a growing acceptance of all components of the regional society, the number of non-Asian observers at such affairs increased. Often there was advance publication of respectful obituaries for deceased Chinese, many of whom had been resident longer than the current Euro-Americans. Among them were Don Man Duck (or Dong Wing Duck), a forty-five-year-old employee of the Annex Restaurant who collapsed on the street because of a fatal stroke; Charley Sie, another Prescott restaurant worker for thirty-five years; Kim Toy, a sixty-year-old Hong Kong woman who had lived in Prescott some twenty-five years; and Lem Wee (or Lean Wee), sixty-seven-year-old asthma victim and long-time member of the local Chinese Masons.[170]

The most detailed account of such a funeral appeared in the *Prescott Journal Miner* of August 25, 1908.

167. City of Prescott, Death Records, 1899–1903, vol. 1.
168. *Arizona Journal Miner*, February 8, 1908.
169. Mortuary records, Archives, Sharlot Hall Museum.
170. *Arizona Journal Miner*, August 22, November 20, 1908; March 5, December 1909.

[Figure 16] The novelty of Chinese funerals, which usually spilled out into Granite Street, generally attracted a few onlookers, as well as Chinese mourners. At right is a table with a few typical food offerings which accompany the deceased. At left the hearse awaits the slow drive to the Citizens' Cemetery located on a low hill east of town. The burial would remain undisturbed until a team of Chinese grave diggers arrived in Arizona Territory and exhumed all accumulated remains of their countrymen in order to ship them back to China. *Courtesy* Goldwater Collection, Arizona Historical Foundation.

Although not as ostentatious as similar events following the death of Chinese of high degree among their countrymen here, the funeral of Chung Sack, Sunday afternoon at 4:30 o'clock, was still pageant in effect. The rites, strictly Oriental, occupied half an hour in front of the Joss house before the procession started to the Citizens Cemetery. The usual burning of incense and punks attended the chanting of the funeral services, intelligible to few outside of the bequeued natives of the land who consider a mixture of rice and roast pig washed down with a decoction of unadulterated tea the richest of delicacies. Chung Sack was not of the mandarin stock, so the ears of the curious Occidents present at his funeral were not deafened by the clashing of cymbals and the music of the

Chinese band which kept the evil one, according to Chinese traditions, from attending other funeral marches.

However, the dead was well supplied with the usual roast shoat, rice, candles, tea, and chop sticks, to nourish and light him on his long journey. His clothing and personal belongings accompanied the eatables on an express wagon behind the hearse to the cemetery. In the cemetery the bedding and dry goods were converted into ashes and the eatables, apparently contrary to custom, deposited on the coffin. The latter is believed to be precautionary against the removal of the delicacies from the grave in years past by outsiders, thus compelling the spirit of the departed to travel to its heavenly home without food or drink and in the dark.

In some western towns the Chinese dead were segregated into their own cemeteries. In Prescott they shared the community burial grounds on a low hill east of town but were confined to its northeastern corner. Existing records for twenty-six deaths between 1899 and 1912, including that of Chung Sack, indicate preliminary burial there.[171] Unfortunately, desecration of these Chinese graves was not uncommon. One instance was mentioned in the *Arizona Republican* of May 30, 1898:

> Vandals have been operating recently in the Citizens cemetery at Prescott where they have removed the headboards of a number of Chinese graves.

Many of the Chinese had no desire to remain permanently in America while alive, and they definitely did not plan to stay there when dead. Part of their immigration proceedings included arrangements for the return to China of their mortal remains should they die abroad. It was of utmost importance that they were assured of final rest among their ancestors. Having their bones moved one or more times posed no emotional problem; in China itself it was not uncommon to change burial sites in order to attain a more propitious location, based on *feng shui*, or geomancy, the state of the

---

171. City of Prescott, Health Department records; Yavapai County Hospital death records; Ruffner Mortuary death records, Archives, Sharlot Hall Museum.

earth's currents being in complementary alignment.[172] Most Euro-Americans on the frontier knew of the shipment back to the motherland of the Chinese dead. California had passed a disinterment ordinance with fines of one hundred to one hundred fifty dollars for shipping human remains to China.[173] Such a ruling was not made in Arizona. The exact way in which this movement of the dead was accomplished, probably a mystery to most Euro-Americans, was graphically described by an early California observer.

> In about five months, little or nothing will be left of the body but dust and bones, as Chinamen decay very quickly here. The information of the death of John will have been transmitted to of the officers of the company to which he belonged in San Francisco. There are four companies. Each have two or three men, whose business it is to travel over the State, making proper calculations for decomposition, and gather up the relics of their late members. At the proper time, the persons appointed will come to Stockton and make the proper application for disinterment. They take from the box . . . the longest bone, say the leg, get a box made of that length, and 18 inches or 2 feet wide and deep, for the reception of all the bones. Each bone is then taken out of the large box and dipped into a bucket of brandy and water. They are then polished with a stiff brush until they almost shine, and are then packed closely in the smaller receptacle. The polishers do not touch the bones with their hands, but handle them very dexterously with two sticks. They are very scrupulous in preserving every bone. The small box is then nailed up and addressed to San Francisco, and the bones of the Celestial, in due time, are laid in his native land as per agreement and Chinese law.[174]

The regional press substantiated the existence of this exhumation practice in the Arizona Territory.

> In the express car of the Guaymas train which stopped here [Maricopa] yesterday were 51 small and shallow boxes contain-

172. Chen 1940: 41.

173. Dillon 1962: 16, 103.

174. *San Francisco Evening Bulletin*, June 29, 1861, quoting *Stockton Republican*. Some archaeologists have suggested that human bones were packed in large ceramic jars for shipment to China. Quellmalz 1976: 293.

ing the bones of a corresponding number of Chinamen which are being sent back to China by the Six Companies for burial, according to the contract into which the Companies enter with every Chinese who comes to America. The economical Six Companies, however, lessen the cost of transportation by leaving the bodies buried so long in America that only fragments of the bones are recoverable.[175]

The records of Chinese deaths in Prescott for the territorial period must be incomplete, but they do provide meager insight into one health problem plaguing this segment of the population. Where cause of death was indicated, it most often was consumption or pneumonia and can be attributed to substandard housing. Other respiratory problems such as tuberculosis or influenza, venereal diseases, digestive disorders, and headaches were likely ailments. Convinced of the efficacy of their ancient folk medicine, the local Chinese surely resorted to the rich lore of herbal and other concoctions on which generations of their ancestors had depended. Probably one of the stores along south Granite Street was that of an herbalist, who dispensed promises of restored health from a bank of tiny drawers filled with packets of dried plant and animal remains or glass vials of liquid or powdered medicines. The root ginseng, dug at midnight under a full moon, was the principal all-purpose remedy for a great variety of ills ranging from depression to the weakness of old age. Soybean curd was considered good for jaundice, fennel for hernias or eye catarrhs, shark fins for restoring strength.[176]

According to one frequently-told story, a Chinese cook at a mining camp near Prescott discovered that the woodpile for his kitchen stove harbored a den of rattlesnakes, and he proceeded to catch them. He cut them into pieces, preserved the bits in alcohol, and sold slices to local comrades as a cure for rheumatism.[177] Snake flesh also was considered an aid for vision.[178]

A territorial reporter regaled his readers with a similar oddity, although the intent perhaps was a slur.

175. *Arizona Citizen*, March 8, 1910.
176. Wallnofer and von Rottauscher 1965.
177. *Prescott Courier*, Centennial edition, 1964; Prescott High School student papers, 1949: 19–20. Archives, Sharlot Hall Museum.
178. Wallnofer and von Rottauscher 1965: 172.

We had the pleasure of presenting, this morning, to a Celestial, a beautiful little skunk which we captured with a trap last night. The Chinaman took the destroyer of our poultry to the outer edge of town, prepared a quantity of wood, placed it properly, touched the match and in a few moments the flames were ready to receive his skunkship. The Celestial carefully watched the cremation process, and when the flesh was burned from the bones and the bones reduced to ashes, they were carefully gathered, bottled, and prepared to be sent to China, where they will be placed on the shelf of some eminent physician, by him to be used in some way for the cure of the dreaded, disgusting and nauseating disease of leprosy, so prevalent in the old world. People needn't wonder hereafter what skunks were made for.[179]

Illness and disease among the Prescott Chinese must have been fairly commonplace, given their unhygienic mode of life. Yet they did not make use of available Euro-American medical facilities. Yavapai County hospital records for the period between 1890 and 1910 and the 1910 federal census list only three Chinese patients: Juay Wong in 1904, Charles Kino in 1907, and Charles Kim in 1910. The Chinese may have distrusted American medical practices or may have been fearful of confinement among persons different from themselves; perhaps they could not afford the associated expense or simply were characteristically fatalistic.[180]

By 1910, the number of Prescott Chinese had dropped to 159, only three percent of the total population.[181] Only a fifth of them claimed to have been born in the United States, and some of those might have been among the persons taking advantage of the loss of government records at San Francisco. The rest were hard-core sojourners. How many would ever attain their dream of a nest egg was problematical. The several octogenarians among them most likely never saw China again. Many were beginning to adopt western clothes and haircuts and were becoming functionally bilingual, but it is unlikely that there had been any meaningful assimilation of American culture. After more than half a century of pressures from both East and West, these men still comprised an alien block.

179. *Arizona Weekly Miner*, November 28, 1879.
180. Lee 1960: 328.
181. U.S. Federal Census, Arizona Territory, 1910.

Included in the 1910 Chinese colony in Prescott were just three women. Two must have been allowed to enter the country as spouses of men describing themselves as nonlaborers although they were cooks. One woman had been born in California. They brought the total number of adult Chinese females documented as having lived in Prescott during any part of the territorial period to twelve, although possibly others had sifted through the tabulation process.

One family stood out from the rest of the colony. A Shina and his wife, He Chag, a California native, were the parents of five children born in Arizona (Figure 17). Whether those births occurred in Prescott is unknown. Their names—Minnie, Annie, Frank, Louisa, and Harold—underscore a deep parental desire to have them grow up as Chinese Americans rather than as offspring of a temporary alien worker in the United States.

The average age of the Chinese group remained at forty-two-plus years, and the range of occupations was similar to what it had been ten years earlier. No new avenues had opened for advancement up the economic ladder. Food services, including cooking, waiting tables, washing dishes, or managing restaurants, still engaged the largest number of Chinese (Table 1). Laundering was a close second occupation. There were just seven merchants, three of them explicitly identified as grocers serving an exclusively Chinese clientele. They were Lim Yee, Lee Yin, and Kaim Hing Yun, and Jim Jung worked as a grocery store clerk. They lived and operated their businesses at 162, 159, 154, and 156 South Granite Street, respectively. Since five stores in a line on the west side of Granite Street appear on a contemporary map (Map 5), two must have been outlets for general merchandise. A letter written by a New York visitor confirms this assumption.

> I think you will like the lily and hope Angeline will be pleased with hers. You can tell her how to fix it. We got them at the Chinese store this morning. I know you would just delight in going in there. There are lots of pretty and curious pieces of china—not very expensive, either—and Chinese baskets, doileys, etc. I mean to bring some pieces of china home if I have any extra money.[182]

182. Letter of November 11, 1908, by Grace C. Drake. Archives, Sharlot Hall Museum.

[Figure 17] The American-born children of Chinese parents, A Shina, a Prescott cook, and He Chag, a native of California, represent a new ethnic group which emerged in the early twentieth century. They are shown about 1910 in the yard of their rented home at 106 North Granite Street, wearing Western clothes. The bow and pigtail of the child on the right resembles the hairstyle of most other little girls in the community. The children's names, Minnie, Annie, Frank, Louisa, and Harold also signal their parents' intention to identify them as Chinese-Americans. *Courtesy* Sharlot Hall Museum.

None of the three women noted in the 1910 census worked as prostitutes. Chinese men had to content themselves with the twenty-six Euro-American, one black, and four Japanese women responsible for an expansion of the "female boarding houses," as the Sanborn mappers called them, from their original locality opposite the joss house to both sides of Granite Street south of Goodwin.

The most significant change from 1900 was that of residence. Only thirty-three Chinese did not live on either south or north Granite Street (Table 2). Yong Sin and his wife, Die, were the sole property owners there, the remainder renting from Euro-American landlords, who generally had not improved their properties for thirty years. No Chinese resided on the rebuilt Whiskey Row, but a laundry with five workers was at 240 North Montezuma Street. Five Chinese men were back at the Officers Row in the reopened Whipple Barracks. Eight were tending gardens in Miller Valley.

The Chee Kung Tong, or Chinese Masons, still was the focal element of social life. The Grand Master of the society included the Prescott order in a 1910 visit.[183]

According to the 1910 census, the Chinese remained the most sizable minority group in town. In order of numbers, they were followed by blacks and mulattoes (98), Hispanics (84), Japanese (22), Native Americans (3), and Filipinos (2). All filled unskilled or semiskilled jobs, but their competition for those usually held by the Chinese was not excessive. Some black women and Japanese men worked as cooks. Some Hispanic and mulatto women washed clothes. Notwithstanding, there seemed to be a niche for everyone, as outwardly at least, life comfortably flowed from today to tomorrow.

In 1910, despite the provincial air of status quo, great change was in the wind. Arizona passed from territorial status into statehood within two years. The Chinese Empire became the Chinese Republic at almost the same time. Important as these political events on opposite sides of the world were, little immediate effect can be identified within the diminished Prescott Chinese colony, stranded on the outer borderlands of both. The Chinaman's chance in Prescott had not improved in forty years.

EPILOGUE: NOW THE CHINESE ARE GONE

After the 1900 fire, some enterprising Chinese opened eating houses, the so-called noodle joints, in their quarter of town. Their principal customers were those coming out of the neighboring houses of joy. Others continued to work in the restaurants associated with Prescott's many bars. That employment was to cease on December 31, 1914, when Arizona adopted a prohibition law. The saloons went out of business and with them most of the restaurants. The robust bachelor era of drinking and eating on the town had been replaced by mom's home-cooked meals.

During the second decade of the twentieth century, Prescott experienced a greater economic stagnation than ever before and no growth in population. The territorial capital and the revenues it had generated had been lost years earlier. Main intercontinental transportation routes bypassed the town, forestalling introduction of

183. *Arizona Journal Miner*, February 5, 1910.

manufacturing industries. Mining was in a slump. Ranching, long the mainstay, always was uncertain. Fort Whipple had closed permanently as a military post. World War I came and went, with little resulting local prosperity.

With their fortunes geared to those of the Euro-American community, and without the emergence of a stratified social structure within their own ranks which might have meant survival on some levels when other options failed, the discouraged, one-class Chinese slowly pulled up stakes. Some returned to China for the final time, free at last from the haunting specters of inspector and hatchetman. Others sought the security of expanding Chinatowns in the major cities of the west coast. It was of little comfort that they had hung on longer in a rural environment of the mountain West than many of their fellow sojourners.[184] They still were victims of the same economic and racial barriers. For some, their overseas adventure had consumed most of their adult lives and gained them only a limited tolerance from Euro-American associates. The Methodist Church mission school established "to uplift the celestial population of Prescott by means of church endeavors" was sold and dismantled.[185] Joe Ah Jew, for forty years a determined Neo-American, committed voter in all elections, and supporter of many social causes unrelated to his background, sold his Windsor Restaurant and went back to die in the land of his forebears.[186] Had he had a family in Prescott, he would have remained. As it was, a wife and children prohibited from immigrating lured him away. Consequently, Prescott lost one of its few acculturated Chinese of the territorial era. Miller Valley, the area "vegetabled by a clan of Orientals," was platted and subdivided for modest homes.[187] Whipple Barracks, once employer of some Asians, became a Veterans Hospital.

When the Great Depression hit in 1929, there remained just four Chinese laundries in Prescott scattered in places in the central business district other than the original Chinatown. Their days were numbered, as their hand services became luxuries, and their former customers turned either to personal washing machines or to the steam laundry. The Yee Hang Yon Restaurant at 138 South Granite

184. Lee 1949: 422–32.
185. *Arizona Journal Miner*, August 12, 1919.
186. *Arizona Journal Miner*, September 6, 1919.
187. *Arizona Journal Miner*, April 4, 1922.

Street brought in a few Euro-American diners eager for the dishes of yesteryear.[188] Down the street the Quong Hing and Dong Wah groceries served an ethnic market that was steadily evaporating through regrouping into metropolitan Chinatowns or through death. The passage of time had so eroded the hold of tradition that those whose earthly tenure ended in Prescott were buried there permanently.

In 1934 the municipal authorities cut Goodwin Street across Granite Creek and leveled the abandoned shanty town to its south. Several years later Chinatown itself was torn down, Granite Street was paved, and all tangible signs of the former Chinese presence were sealed under new buildings and surfaced parking lots. After a street-widening project during the 1950s, there remained only five Chinese graves in the old Citizens Cemetery, their weathered head-stones thrust askew by vandals and the elements.[189] Over a period of seventy years, the lifespan of the Arizona Territory and the three following decades, perhaps as many as five hundred Chinese had passed through Prescott. All arrived with high hopes, but some died halfway around the world from their ancestors and others departed disheartened. They had been as phantoms in a fleeting parade, now scarcely remembered by the local white Americans or the few Chinese Americans who came after World War II to replace them. ✤

---

188. Prescott City Directory, 1930.

189. According to data in the archives at the Sharlot Hall Museum, the headstones belonged to the graves of Jim Lee, died 1915?; Charles Lo, died 1930; Guon Guy, died 1931; Leung Lee Fong (Fund), died 1931; and Hee Sing, died 1929. However, except for partial determination of what appear to be some memorials and names of native villages in China, other translators have been unable to confirm these names. Six graves with headstones bearing inscriptions in Chinese characters are at the out-of-town burial site to which remains were taken during the 1950s. Inasmuch as the readable dates there are 1941, 1942, and 1950, it is assumed that the original graves were in the most northerly sector of Citizens Cemetery.

REFERENCES

Unpublished Sources

National Archives, Los Angeles Branch
    Chinese Exclusion Case Files, 1897–1911, Third and Fourth Judicial
      District, Arizona Territory
    Criminal Case Files, 1891–1911, Third and Fourth Judicial District,
      Arizona Territory
    U. S. Register of Actions, Chinese Exclusion Docket Book, Fourth
      Judicial District, Arizona Territory

Prescott, City of
    Death Records, 1899–1903
    Health Department records

Sharlot Hall Museum, Archives
    Churches folder
    Groom Map, 1864
    Letters
    Mortuary records
    Mortuary records, Ruffner Mortuary
    Obituaries
    Prescott High School student papers
    Village of Prescott, Ordinances
    Yavapai County Hospital records

Yavapai County Court House
    Minute Record of Orders of Naturalization, 1865–Sept. 13, 1906
    Register of Criminal Actions, Third Judicial District Court, Proceed-
      ings, June 1894

U.S. Federal Census
    Arizona Territory, 1864, 1870, 1880, 1900, 1910

Newspapers

    Arizona Citizen (Tucson), 1910
    Arizona Daily Star (Tucson), 1884, 1935
    Arizona Journal Miner (Prescott), 1876–1922
    Arizona Republican (Phoenix), 1898–99

Arizona Weekly Miner (Prescott), 1869–90
Enterprise (Prescott), 1877–86
Howler (Prescott), 1900
Phoenix Daily Enterprise, 1904
Prescott Courier, 1964
Prescott Journal Miner, 1908
Prescott Morning Courier, 1886–96
Prescott Weekly Courier, 1882
San Francisco Chronicle, 1893
San Francisco Evening Bulletin, 1861

Secondary Sources

Allen, J. S.
    1941   "Yavapai Inferno: The Story of the Great Prescott
               Fire." *Arizona Highways*, May.
Bluden, Caroline, and Mark Elvin
    1983   *Cultural Atlas of China*. New York: Facts on File.
Bret Harte, John
    1980   *Portrait of a Desert Pueblo*. Woodland Hills, Calif.:
               Windsor.
Chang, K. C.
    1977   *Food in Chinese Culture: Anthropological and Histor-
               ical Interpretations*. New Haven: Yale University
               Press.
Chen, Ta
    1940   *Emigrant Communities in South China*. English edi-
               tion by Bruno Lasket. New York: Institute of Pacific
               Relations.
Clayre, Alasdair
    1984   *The Heart of the Dragon*. Boston: Houghton Mifflin.
Clyde, Paul H., and Burton F. Beers
    1966   *A History of the Far East, of the Western Impact and
               the Eastern Response (1830–1965)*. Englewood Cliffs,
               N.J.: Prentice-Hall.
Culin, Stewart
    1890a   "Chinese Secret Societies in the United States." *Jour-
               nal of American Folk-Lore*, Vol. 3, No. 1, 39–43.
    1890b   "Customs of the Chinese in America." *Journal of
               American Folk-Lore*, Vol. 3, No. 1, 191–200.

1891   "The Gambling Games of the Chinese in America." *Publications of the University of Pennsylvania, Series in Philology, Literature, and Archaeology,* Vol. 1, No. 4.

1970   *The I'Hing or "Patriotic Rising," a Secret Society Among the Chinese in America.* San Francisco: R & E Research Associates.

Dai, Bingham

1964   "Opium Addiction: A Socio-psychiatric Approach." In *Contributions to Urban Sociology,* edited by Ernest W. Burgess and Donald J. Bogue, pp. 643–54. Chicago: University of Chicago Press.

Davis, Fei-Lung

1971   *Primitive Revolutionaries of China.* Honolulu: University Press of Hawaii.

Dicker, Laverne Mau

1979   *The Chinese in San Francisco: A Pictorial History.* New York: Dover.

Dillon, Richard H.

1962   *The Hatchet Men: The Story of the Tong Wars in San Francisco's Chinatown.* New York: Coward-McCann.

Dun, J. Li

1965   *The Ageless Chinese: A History.* New York: Charles Scribner.

Fong, Laurence Michael

1980   "Sojourners and Settlers: The Chinese Experience in Arizona." Reprinted with different pagination (1–86) from *Journal of Arizona History,* Vol. 21, No. 2, 22–56.

1984   "Desert Crossing: Migrations and Settlements of Early Chinese in Arizona." *Papers of the Second National Conference on Chinese American Studies,* 1980, San Francisco, pp. 198–99.

Gernet, Jacques

1982   *A History of Chinese Civilization.* Cambridge: Cambridge University Press.

Greenwood, Roberta S.

1980   "The Chinese on Main Street." In *Archaeological Perspectives on Ethnicity in America,* edited by Robert L. Schuyler, pp. 113–23. Farmingdale, N.Y.: Baywood.

Hall, Beverly
    1980   "Hey, Chinaman, Do You Speak English?" Manuscript, Arizona Historical Foundation, Arizona State University, Tempe.

Hoy, William
    1942   *The Chinese Six Companies*. San Francisco: Chinese Consolidated Benevolent Association.

Kane, Harry Hubbell
    1976   *Opium-smoking in America and China*. New York: Arno.

Kraus, George
    1969   "Chinese Laborers and the Construction of the Central Pacific." *Utah Historical Quarterly*, Vol. 37, No. 1, 41–57.

Lee, Rose Hum
    1948   "Social Institutions of a Rocky Mountain Chinatown." *Social Forces*, Vol. 27, No. 1, 1–11.
    1949   "The Decline of Chinatowns in the United States." *American Journal of Sociology*, Vol. 54, 422–32.
    1960   *The Chinese in the United States of America*. Hong Kong: Hong Kong University Press.

Light, Ivan H.
    1972   *Ethnic Enterprise in America: Business and Welfare Among Chinese, Japanese, and Blacks*. Berkeley: University of California Press.

Lyman, Stanford M.
    1970   *The Asian in the West*. Social Science and Humanities Pub. No. 4, Desert Research Institute, University of Nevada, Reno.
    1974   *Chinese Americans*. New York: Random House.

Olsen, John W.
    1983   "An Analysis of East Asian Coins Excavated in Tucson, Arizona." *Historical Archaeology*, Vol. 71, No. 2, 41–55.

Ong, Paul
    1983   "Chinese Laundries as an Urban Occupation in Nineteenth-Century California." *Annals of the Chinese Historical Society of the Pacific Northwest*, 68–85.

Parker, Charles Franklin
    1941   "Chinee Boy." *Arizona Highways*, September.

Perkins, Clifford
    1984   "Recollections of a Chinese-Immigration Inspector." In *Arizona Memories*, edited by Anne Hodges Morgan and Rennard Strickland, pp. 217–32. Tucson: University of Arizona Press.

Potter, Alvina N.
    1964   *The Many Lives of the Lynx: A Century of Mining on Lynx Creek between 1863 and 1963*. Prescott: n.p.

Prazniak, Roxann
    1984   "The Chinese in Woodland, California." In *The Chinese Laundry on Second Street: Papers on Archaeology at the Woodland Opera House Site*, California Archaeological Reports No. 24, pp. 121–38. Sacramento: California Department of Parks and Recreation.

Quellmalz, Carl Robert
    1976   "Late Chinese Provincial Export Wares." *Oriental Art*, n.s., Vol. 22, No. 3, 289–98.

Rohe, Randall E.
    1982   "After the Gold Rush: Chinese Mining in the Far West, 1850–1890." *Montana: The Magazine of Western History*, Vol. 32, No. 4, 2–19.

Siu, Paul E. P.
    1952   "The Sojourner." *American Journal of Sociology*, Vol. 58, No. 1, 34–44.
    1964   "The Isolation of the Chinese Laundryman." In *Contributions to Urban Sociology*, edited by Ernest W. Burgess and Donald J. Bogue, pp. 429–42. Chicago: University of Chicago Press.

Spier, Robert E. G.
    1958   "Food Habits of Nineteenth-Century California Chinese." *California Historical Society Quarterly*, Vol. 37, No. 1, 79–84; Vol. 37, No. 2, 129–36.

Strobridge, William F.
    1984   "Chinese in the Spanish American War and Beyond." *Papers of the Second National Conference on Chinese American Studies*, 1980, San Francisco, pp. 13–15.

Tsai, Shih-shan Henry
    1983   *China and the Overseas Chinese in the United States, 1868–1911*. Fayetteville: University of Arkansas Press.

Walker, Henry P., and Don Bufkin
    1979   *Historical Atlas of Arizona*. Norman: University of Oklahoma Press.

Wallnofer, Heinrich, and Anna von Rottauscher
    1965   *Chinese Folk Medicine*. New York: Crown.
Wegars, Priscilla
    1984   "Besides Polly Bemis: Historical and Artifactural Evidence for Chinese Women in the West, 1848–1930." Paper presented at annual meeting of the Society for Historical Archaeology, Sacramento.
Wei Min She Labor Committee
    1974   *Chinese Working People in America*. San Francisco: United Front Press.
Weisberger, Bernard A.
    1970   *The American People*. New York: American Heritage.
Wells, Mariann Kaye
    1971   *Chinese Temples in California*. San Francisco: R & E Research Associates.
Yap, Yong, and Arthur Cottrell
    1977   *Chinese Civilization: From the Ming Revival to Chairman Mao*. London: Weinfeld & Nicolson.
Yoder, Phillip D.
    1951   "The History of Fort Whipple." Master's thesis, University of Arizona, Tucson.

Reviews of Recent Books

Albuquerque: Coming Back to the U.S.A. By Margaret Randall. Vancouver: New Star Books, 1986. 350 pp. $12.95 paper.

Borderlands/La Frontera: The New Mestiza. By Gloria Anzaldúa. San Francisco: Spinsters/Aunt Lute Book Company, 1987. 203 pp. $8.95 paper.

A Breeze Swept Through. By Luci Tapahonso. Albuquerque: West End Press, 1987. 51 pp. $5.95 paper.

Margaret Randall, Gloria Anzaldúa, and Luci Tapahonso have produced studies of the psychic meanings of leaving home, of crossing the boundary between the familiar and the strange, the acceptable and the deviant. Although they work in different genres and speak from different cultures and generations, the threads uniting their narratives are tied to the specific biophysical environment of the American Southwest (or Mexican North). This tie mediates the very different experiences they have with the classic journey away from home and back again.

Margaret Randall's *Albuquerque* is a journal of her first year back in the United States after a long period living and working in Latin America. Randall grew up in Albuquerque in the 1950s, when the town was beginning to grow with the influx of federal funds and eastern immigrants of the postwar period. Daughter of middle-class, liberal parents, Randall remembers her teenage attempts to at once fit into the social life of burgeoning Anglo-dominated suburbs and yet resist racist housing and schooling policies. Returning to Albuquerque after an absence of many years, she struggled to locate the old neighborhoods that have been replaced by the distinctive urban sprawl of a western city. Albuquerque retains its meaning, however, as a specific biophysical environment. Much of the journal is dedicated to the story of her new home—built of adobe in the foothills of the Sandia Mountains, it embodies all the physical characteristics of the Southwest important to her.

Margaret Randall returned to the Southwest after years writing about and photographing the impact of political upheaval on the lives of powerless people—women and children especially—in Latin America. Although the physical landscapes of Albuquerque are not unique, she also realizes that the city does not exist in isolation from the rest of the country. Middle-class values, consumer economics, racism, and sexism reign in the Southwest as much as in New York City or rural Washington State. For Randall, the worst experience is to discover that her years in Latin America earned her the scrutiny of the Immigration and Naturalization Service (INS), which questioned her petition for a re-granting of American citizenship, in part because of her publications. *Albuquerque* provides a wrenching account of her efforts to regain citizenship.

Randall attempts, in *Albuquerque*, to substitute personal experience of place for socially defined boundaries of state or nation. In coming home to Albuquerque, she hoped to come home to a place in which topography is more important than politics, in which the biophysical landscape is redemptive and has priority over the social construction of lines marking off cities, states, and countries. But, the journal documents the difficulty of the effort as boundaries established by social custom and law intrude. The problem with Randall's evocation of Albuquerque is how little a part the place actually plays in her narrative. Recently returned, burdened with the battle for citizenship and the need to earn money on lecture tours, Randall seems to have had scant time to really contemplate what day-to-day life in the city means.

In *Borderlands/La Frontera*, Gloria Anzaldúa explores a tension similar to Randall's: between her love for the landscape of her native people's original homeland, and her resistance to sexist strictures both within her own culture and emanating from Anglo culture. Expanding on the concept of borders, Anzaldúa shows how all sorts of boundaries restrict personal freedom: from the political edge between the United States and Mexico, to the gender split between men and women and sexual divisions between straights and gays; from religious differences between Catholicism and native beliefs, to battles over the rights of the community versus those of the individual, culminating in each individual's psychic split between the conscious and unconscious. In *Borderlands/La Frontera*, Anzaldúa, in the persona of the *mestiza* who is the result of crossbreeding, situates herself literally in mid-stream, at the crossing point from one duality to another. At this point, she argues, the border disappears and unity becomes possible.

The first person in six generations to leave her South Texas valley home, Anzaldúa chronicles her reasons for leaving. Mingling history, personal narrative, and poetry, the book recounts the waves of colonialism which created ever-shifting political boundaries in the region along the Texas-Mexico border. It also describes her own family's poverty and mistreatment as mixed-blood people living on that border, and her personal struggles within a strongly traditional community unable to cope with either her individual ambition or her lesbianism.

Anzaldúa's book argues that her personal experience, her family and community inheritance, and the history of her people all serve to place her on the border, representative of a new sort of culture. Like Randall, who returned to Albuquerque that was home and not home, Anzaldúa returned home acknowledging that she would always be both one of the community and an outsider. In "Nopalitos" she writes of her differences with her community: "I have more languages than they,/ am aware of every root of my *pueblo;*/ they, my people, are not./ They are the living, sleeping roots" (113). What unites her to them, however, is the land. Although she offers a harsh vision of what it means to be a field worker in the arid Southwest, in the end the physical landscape is the unifying link to a society she views with some ambivalence. The boundaries which "split" her flesh are embedded in her land, the land of her people: "This is my home/this thin edge of/barbwire./ But the skin of the earth is seamless"(3). What Randall experiences as a split—the break between the destructive culture of Albuquerque and the redemptive physical landscape of the place—Anzaldúa reconciles. Anzaldúa presents herself as engaged in a continuous journey out and back, constantly leaving and returning. In this motion between home and outside lies her ability to reconcile the appositions and overcome the boundaries.

Anzaldúa is an accomplished writer, able to marshall passionate intensity in support of her attempt to do away with dualities. Although she sometimes overstates her case, as in the contention that "colored homosexuals have more knowledge of other cultures; have always been in the forefront . . . of all liberation struggles in this country" (85), *Borderlands/La Frontera* is a gripping argument for the demolition of many of the artificial borders dividing people of the region.

Luci Tapahonso's *A Breeze Swept Through* articulates even more consciously than Anzaldúa the redemptive qualities of cyclic motion. *A Breeze Swept Through* is a collection of poems recounting Tapahonso's life in towns like Shiprock and Albuquerque. Once, and in many ways still a migratory people, Navajo writers situate much of their writing on the road. Heroines in Tapahonso's poems seem to have considerably more psychic and physical freedom than the girls and women depicted in Randall's Albuquerque or Anzaldúa's South Texas pueblo. When they leave home, they run *to* something rather than away *from* a restricted life. So, in "Last Year the Pinons Were Plentiful" a woman leaves her husband, heading for the hills with a stranger, but her leaving is redemptive: the following year the pinon nuts are bountiful.

Tapahonso's poetry is much less concerned with the political boundaries which cause Randall and Anzaldúa so much pain. Her poetry chronicles the more personalized reasons people have for leaving home, or coming back—a failed marriage, a new job, the birth of a child. Finding more support for who she is in her culture, Tapahonso spends little time recounting the internal tensions of one who in leaving is rejecting community values, and in coming back is again at odds with her culture. Further, she does not present herself as only the prodigal—returning with a critical message to those rooted in the land. In Tapahonso's more cyclic motion, the one returning can also, and at any time, be the one left behind. The point, as she beautifully recounts in "For Misty Starting School," is to have a proper ritual for maintaining the ties across the distance.

Finally, in Tapahonso's poems there is very little opposition between Navajo culture and the land on which the people live. In "Come Into The Shade" she answers the question "Where do you come from?" with a description which begins with the land—"Hard summer rains/ leave hollow beads/ of moisture in the dust,"—and ends with a family party— "We'll just get some mutton/ at the trading post and cook it/ under the trees here" (3). Of the three books, Tapahonso's comes closest to consistently evoking daily life in New Mexico. Sharing Anzaldúa's burned-in knowledge that life in a poverty-stricken, exploited situation can be dangerous and degrading, she is still able to provide a clear, unambiguous account of her deep attachment to the place.

Finally, the titles of these three books reflect the extent to which borders impact on the authors. Randall, caught in the midst of a battle to regain her right to live in a specific country, titles her book with the name of a place, a place with a specific social and political history. Anzaldúa, seeking reconcilation between the many dualities in her life, grounds her title in appositions—using both the Spanish and English terms for a political boundary existing anywhere edges meet. Tapahonso, centered most strongly within the land and her culture, chooses a title least expressive of a specific place, but most evocative of what it means to live in the high deserts of the South-west. Taken together the books exemplify a fact long known by writers attempting to define the Southwest—describing the physical qualities of the region is relatively easy, determining its boundaries is trickier, constrained as the determination is by any individual's cultural history of tenancy on the land.

American Studies   VERA NORWOOD
University of New Mexico
Albuquerque, New Mexico

The Legacy of Conquest: The Unbroken Past of the American West. By
    Patricia Nelson Limerick. New York: W. W. Norton & Company,
    1987. 396 pp. $17.95 cloth, $9.95 paper.

Just before being asked to review this book, I attended a lecture, "Misconceptions of the American West" given by Patricia Nelson Limerick, which made me eager to read her book, *The Legacy of Conquest.* To prove her points, she illustrated the book and the lecture well with interesting anecdotes about situations and people from both the distant and the recent history of the American West. According to Limerick, she intends this book for a general audience, to dispel the mythical vision of the American West as only a place of "freedom, opportunity, abundance, and success"; in contrast, historians see the West as a place of "conflict, unintended consequences, and complexities" (324). This disparity between the popular notion of the West and the historical reality has distorted thought processes so that there is little understand-ing of the origins of modern problems. This history is intended as a valuable aid for government and business leaders who are not conscious that what happened *then* has a bearing on what happens *now.*

Limerick's personal experiences have made her aware of the per-vasiveness of the old "wild west" myth. Often strangers inquire about her profession, and when she replies that she teaches "History of the American West," invariably the response is, "Oh, what fun!" This is a response that appalls Limerick, whose dominant images of the West are more apt to include the Sand Creek and Ludlow massacres, the Nevada-Test-Site fallout, or the Japanese internment camps than scenes from John Wayne movies or passages from romantic western novels such as *The Virginian* or those written by Louis L'Amour.

Her purpose in writing the book goes beyond knowledge for knowledge's sake. At the lecture, she revealed that her understanding of mythology has broadened after viewing Bill Moyers's interviews with Joseph Campbell in the recent PBS television series "The Power of Myth." The word "myth" as used in scholarship today no longer connotes only false ideas. The pervasiveness, strength, and need for myth as an embodiment of our cultural ideas are beginning to become clear. Mythology seems to be a necessity of mankind as it expresses human yearnings, ambitions, and universal ideals.

As Limerick began to write, her purpose was to destroy and disprove popular misconceptions of the old West. Her mission now is to replace an outdated concept with a "truer" mythology. Those who read *The Legacy of Conquest* will be able to form a new mythology by Limerick's carefully documented argument, her numerous and insightful examples, and her well-written prose. If an American West mythology is necessary, we should base it on historical accuracy or we will all suffer the consequences of decisions based on false information. The new mythology need not be totally negative. It is possible "to celebrate the Western past," realizing that "the brutal massacres come back along with the cheerful barn raisings, the shysters come back with the saints, contracts broken come back with contracts fulfilled" (330).

Limerick's *Legacy of Conquest* offers us a replacement for the images of the Old West we carry in our minds from Saturday afternoon cowboy films. It offers a "revived version of Western history" using the scholarship of individuals who have studied "urban, social, business, labor, Chicano, Indian, or environmental" issues (30). Seeing these issues as a western historian, Limerick combined the research and has created a modern history of the American West, a history as it is being taught in many universities today but a much different history than the average citizen recalls.

This modern account observes western history as acted out by more than the white male trailblazer, settler, or prospector. How did the women of the West survive? What is the Indians' perspective of the "taming of the West"? How does one connect, interrelate, and interpret the history of Hispanic America as a part of western history? What is the story of the Chinese and Japanese within the story of the frontier? The Mormons were also participants in this chronicle as were blacks; the Wobblies and the Ludlow strikers were yet another part. In reference to the popular idea that the West was a place "to get away from it all," Limerick comments: "The West was not where we escaped each other, but where we all met" (291). Limerick does not discuss any of these topics extensively. In fact, a general knowledge of western history or a good reference book would be helpful for background since this is not a survey but "an interpretation and a synthesis" (30). Limerick provides an excellent bibliography which clearly categorizes material for further reading.

Relating the past to the present is a goal that Limerick achieves masterfully. This is not a western history book that ends with 1890, the year Frederick Jackson Turner declared as the closing of the frontier. Because of belief in this arbitrary division, twentieth-century westerners have separated themselves from their past so that they have difficulty believing that they share common problems and experiences with their ancestors. The subtitle of the book, *The Unbroken Past of the American West*, signals an effort to change people's perceptions so that they can hurdle the obstacle Turner and others have placed in human minds, dividing the past from the present. One instance of commonality is the farming situation then and now. "Western farmers in the late nineteenth century lived with a sense of being squeezed by history, in a vise built by dropping prices on one side and high costs on the other" (130–131). Western farmers in the late twentieth century can relate to their antecedents.

This is a history that continues the discussion into today. Erudite decisions need to be made in the West by the public, by government, and by business leaders. Topics that have historical roots include mining, labor problems, water disputes, and controversy over preservation and conservation. Many front-page headlines today deal with complexities that have a historical background. What should be the policy toward fires in Yellowstone Park? Should we declare English an official language? How does one evaluate President Reagan's comments on past Indian policy? How should we resolve Mexican border problems?

> When politicians in the 1980s bemoaned the fact that America had 'lost control' of its border with Mexico, they dreamed up a lost age of mastery. In fact, from the Gulf of Mexico to the Pacific Ocean, the Mexican border was a social fiction that neither nature nor people in search of opportunity observed. (251)

Instead of perpetuating a false myth, we must form a myth based on truth that will serve us rather than defeat us. Patricia Limerick demonstrates that, to begin to solve the dilemmas of the twentieth-century West, we must first know how it all came to be.

English Department
Colorado State University
Fort Collins, Colorado

CAMILLE BAMFORD

Escape from Death Valley, As Told by William Lewis Manly and Other '49ers. Researched, edited, and annotated by LeRoy Johnson and Jean Johnson. Reno: University of Nevada Press, 1987. $26.95 cloth, $15.95 paper.

If Hollywood had made a film biography of William Lewis Manly, John Wayne would not have wanted the part. "The Duke" might have found the plot of two single men rescuing two families from Death Valley to be an appealing one, but the details would surely have diminished his enthusiasm.

In 1849, struggling to escape the desert, Manly did not have the option of riding a spirited horse in the classic western manner. On the contrary, he and the rest of his party walked; the only ones who rode were two malnourished, fretful, small children packed into sidebags on a faithful, but distinctly unglamorous old ox. Manly, moreover, did not have occasion to make much use of John Wayne's favorite fruit of the industrial revolution, the firearm. Death Valley offered Manly next to nothing in the way of game for hunting, and, more important, no "bad guys" would step forward and accept, through the judicious application of gunpowder and metal, the responsibility for the misadventure that had befallen the families. Further, Manly failed, in any number of ways, to meet the standards for tough western masculinity; repeatedly, he despaired, and on a number of occasions, he wept, openly and without shame. Perhaps most damaging for any movie potential, the plot came to no clear end. Manly and his friend John Rogers succeeded in getting the Bennett and Arcan families to Southern California, and then everyone dispersed into Northern California, and everyone ended up working in ordinary ways in ordinary places. There was no discovery of great fortune, there was certainly no "shoot-out," and there was no rising medley of trail music as the sun set in the West.

By the standards of Hollywood and popular fiction, the Gold Rush experiences of Manly, Rogers, the Bennetts, and the Arcans present rather thin gruel. But by nearly any other standard of narrative merit, this story is one of extraordinary power. No wonder LeRoy Johnson and Jean Johnson, a forest geneticist and a cellist and scientific editor, took the story on as something close to a family obsession. The Johnsons' interests came to focus on the question of geography, on ascertaining the route by which Manly and Rogers traveled from the desert to coastal California; the route by which they returned to the families; and the route by which the whole party then traveled out of the desert and into a country that was, in Manly's words, "the most beautiful natural picture a human being ever saw . . . a thousand-acre green meadow, speckled with cattle of all sizes and colors, some lying down and some standing to crop the rich green grass" (136–7). Coastal California has never looked better, before or since.

Using a "scientific method" to weigh the various sources and their sometimes conflicting claims, the Johnsons invested many vacations and many footsteps in the project of choosing the most likely route of the Manly/Bennett party. This book presents their conclusions, with clear maps and equally clear text. Confusion and some controversy have attended the question of the party's various routes in and out of Death Valley. The Johnsons' thorough work should resolve much of this uncertainty.

With this book, the Johnsons also performed the service of reprinting and annotating Manly's earlier version of the story, serialized in the *Santa Clara Valley* in 1888. Since the Johnsons make a persuasive argument that Manly had the assistance of a ghostwriter in assembling his 1894 *Death Valley in '49*, making the 1888 version available is an important service. The Johnsons also include writings from other Death Valley '49ers, John Rogers, Louis Nusbaumer, and James Brier.

This historical episode may lack the ingredients for a proper western adventure film, but it makes for first-rate western prose. William Lewis Manly was not only an authentic hero in his loyalty to the beleaguered Bennett and Arcan families, he also had an enormous gift as a vernacular writer. One almost wishes that the more high-toned literary critics, who are in the habit of celebrating Mark Twain's inauguration of a vernacular voice in *The Adventures of Huckleberry Finn*, would take a turn with Lewis Manly—to explore the question of why it is that Twain and others get enormous credit for imitating the voices of the folk in literature, when the folk who used their own voices in written form do not get much in the way of either recognition or praise. Consider, for instance, the passage in which Manly describes the concrete meaning of encouragement, in their walk out of the valley.

> The women when they reached camp lay down at once, for their work in walking was almost more than they could endure, and when they got up toward night to eat they looked bad enough and could hardly stand upon their sore feet and tired limbs. They would say every night that they would not try to worry through, and would stop and die right there but for the faith they had in Rogers and myself who knew the road, and speaking so confidently of it gave them courage to make another effort. (124)

In its unpretentious phrasing and vivid honesty, Lewis Manly's prose makes a compelling argument for expanding the "Hall of Fame of

Literary Merit" to include those who never once thought of themselves as professional writers or artists, but who were nonetheless pushed by an extraordinary experience into placing on the page words that can nearly burn the reader with their intensity.

On this count, the Johnsons are, understandably, a bit more timid than Manly was. Even though they were clearly gripped—and gripped for years—by this story, they do not tell us why. Perhaps they did not want to run any risk of pushing Manly, Rogers, the Bennetts, and the Arcans out of their rightful position at center stage. But readers might nonetheless wonder: why did a couple in the mid-to-late-twentieth century become so preoccupied with an event in the mid-nineteenth century that they devoted their own free time to tracking the event and its participants? If nothing else, the answer to the question would be an illuminating case study in the power of history, in the ways in which the experience of individuals long-dead can become immediate, authentic, and even inspirational. How did it feel to walk in the footsteps of Lewis Manly and John Rogers? The Johnsons evidently know, but they are not telling.

History Department
University of Colorado
Boulder, Colorado

Patricia Nelson Limerick

Red Hole in Time. By Muriel Marshall. College Station: Texas A & M University Press, 1988. 299 pp. $29.50 cloth, $12.95 paper.

Judging from the number of titles that appear each year, writing local history is a thriving business, but the quality of the books and articles produced is, as one might expect, very uneven. Much local history is still produced by amateur book committees established to commemorate an important anniversary, or by a self-appointed family historian. The works they produce are generally poorly organized pastiches of anecdotes, boosterish and laudatory in interpretation, heavily oriented toward the recording of "firsts" and focused on the pioneer period, and larded with lists and photographs of important people. Many are published in very limited editions, sold by subscription, and produced in gaudy format by vanity presses that exist to prey upon such projects.

Others are fully worthy of the term "history" in a professional sense. Often inspired by the interest in local and family history generated by the bicentennial celebration and Alex Haley's *Roots*, guided by the excellent publications of the American Association for State and Local History, funded by local humanities councils, based on wide-ranging research in documentary and oral sources, written critically and felicitously, and published by academic or responsible private presses, such local studies have enabled us to make giant strides in understanding American history at the grass-roots level.

Though Muriel Marshall has one foot in each stream, most of her weight is on the one placed in the new local historiography. Few historians at any level can write as well as she does. As a former newspaper editor, she stands squarely in the tradition of journalists-turned-historians like Allan Nevins and Bruce Catton, whose ability to turn the bare facts of history into genuine drama often surpasses that of academically trained scholars. Her journalistic background also becomes evident in her willingness to supplement her limited documentary sources with oral interviews and repeated visits, camera in hand, to the sites she discusses to understand the shaping forces of geology and geography.

Her subject is Escalante Canyon on the Uncompaghre Plateau in western Colorado, a beautiful and almost inaccessible setting for her story of cowboys, sheepherders, homesteaders, bootleggers, gunslingers, and an almost indescribably varied cast of other characters who found in the canyon economic opportunity, social escape, and other attractions which an isolated locale could offer. Her characters march across her pages in a wonderful panorama, revealing themselves to us through deftly chosen anecdotes and diary quotations, until their unique personalities and the quality of the lives they were able to wrest from their recalcitrant environment become vividly real.

Marshall's photographs (one assumes they are hers, since they are attributed to no one else) deserve a special word. They could almost stand alone as a pictorial essay on life in Escalante Canyon but that they complement her text so perfectly, and one would miss the narrative depth such a divorce would lose. There are none of the portraits of participants in the narrative which readers of traditional local history almost inevitably expect, but, while we would like to see what some of the people we meet looked like, we have something even better. Marshall knows how to use a camera with a feeling for the setting in which her history takes place. Such photographs assume a narrative power of their own; one remembers James Agee's warning that Walker Evans's photographs in their classic *Let Us Now Praise Famous Men* are not illustrative—they tell their own story. Some readers may wonder that there are no color photographs used to depict a country which Marshall says is spectacularly beautiful, but such readers need to look again, and to learn that black-and-white photography is fully capable of depicting the beauty of such country. What one would lose in the literalness of color one gains in black-and-white's texture and form. Black-and-white photography also enables the publisher to use a great many more photographs within a reasonable production cost.

What a pity, then, that with such rich research, such inherently interesting material on an almost unknown subject, and such effective anecdotes and photographs, that Marshall cannot seem to make this story add up to what it should, The whole is less than the sum of its parts; the parts are the whole story. This unfortunate lack of overall meaning is a result, in the first place, of a mysterious organizational principle that keeps the narrative from moving. *Red Hole in Time* is absolutely innocent of chronology, so there is no development of the community. We know, from Marshall's biographical sketches and anecdotes, that such development was taking place, that Escalante Canyon in 1940 was very different from what it was in 1890, but she offers no comprehensive sense of the nature of that development. There are, of course, other principles of organization available to the historian of such a community, and Marshall's narrative suggests any number of potentially useful themes. But she presents her characters almost at random, seemingly as they popped into her mind or surfaced in her stack of note cards. The result is a high degree of entertainment, particularly as couched in Marshall's wonderful prose, but little in the way of answering the larger questions the historian properly asks.

Perhaps sensing the need for a theme to tie the story together, Marshall chooses the story of a shootout between a colorful Robin-Hood-sort of fellow, Ben Lowe, and the lawman Cash Sampson, in which both men were killed. It is an unfortunate choice. The confrontation does contain a distillation of some of the larger elements in the history of the community such as livestock rustling versus law and order, and Lowe does stand effectively as a symbol for the devil-may-care frontier freedom, while the stolid Sampson represents stable community virtues. But Marshall asks the episode to bear more than it can, for she is unable to bring enough of the rich detail of the canyon's history into focus on those two characters.

Marshall keeps raising our expectations through offhand references that something big is coming. We think she is holding an ace-high straight. But when the last chapter comes, and the chips are on the table, she finally comes down with it, and it is nothing but a pair of deuces. So Tombstone, in one brief moment, came to Escalante Canyon; so what?

Red Hole in Time, then, for all its undeniable virtues, ultimately fails to transcend completely the Podunk-Centennial-Book-Committee-type of local history. It is too bad, for in most aspects it is a very fine book. If it merits the extensive criticism I offer here, it is because it is so good that it should have been even better. Marshall clearly has the talent to produce first-rate history, and one hopes to see much more from her.

Curator of Manuscripts   Gary Topping
Utah State Historical Society Library
Salt Lake City, Utah

A Trace of Desert Waters: The Great Basin Story. By Samuel G. Houghton. Salt Lake City: Howe Brothers, 1986. 287 pp. $11.95 paper.

Dr. James Schiel, serving with the Gunnison Expedition surveying the Great Basin in 1853, wrote that "the shadows of small clouds obscuring the morning sun were the only living, moving thing in the landscape, and they seemed to heighten the feeling of utter gloom. If the eye of a man of ancient Greece had seen this sight, he would have located the entrance to the underworld here" (Frederick W. Bachman and William S. Wallace, eds., *The Land Between*. Los Angeles: Westernlore Press, 1957: 100). To a later generation has come an appreciation of this landscape that John Charles Frémont, looking for the magical mythical river that supposedly ran from the Rockies to the Pacific, first identified as a basin of interior drainage. Samuel Houghton's book, *A Trace of Desert Waters*, addresses this great Empty Quarter of the United States, the magnificent landscape left by past and present, the landscape that underlay the great lake systems: Bonneville, Lahontan, and Death Valley.

Houghton's book is a scholarly non-scholarly book, as difficult to review as it is to categorize. It ranges from anthropology to solar energy, John Charles Frémont to isostatic rebound, from Lake Lahontan to horned larks, all hung on a framework of geological history and a tremendous personal affection for the Great Basin. The Great Basin contains the largest of the four deserts of the contiguous United States and probably the least known, still largely empty, with oases of fascination connected by forever sagebrush and salt bush and tomorrow skies, the predominant route of emigrants and explorers going west, just given its first national park in 1987.

I first read *Desert Waters* a few years ago, as I was beginning work on a book about the four major deserts of the United States. Houghton's book provided no scholarly assist *per se* because it is a secondary source, but it did provide an indispensable overview, a wealth of references to follow, and a marvelous resumé of knowledge to date about the great Pleistocene lakes that covered the Great Basin. While walking the salt flats around a newly filled Sevier Lake, I read Houghton's book; while driving across the Alvord Basin and while sweating through the Great Salt Desert, I read Houghton's book. His information was handy and concise, the only reference to provide such comprehensive data in a single volume. To have access to such information elsewhere I would have had to carry a batch of U.S.G.S. papers, dozens of anthropological reports, two tomes (at least) of geology, and innumerable natural history identification books. That it is now available in paperback makes it even more useful in the field. Then I was captured by Houghton's concern for place that comes through the hours of careful research it must have taken to gather data and to write this book; in rereading, I still am.

Houghton was an attorney who died in 1975 before he saw his book published—a poignant detail, for this book, more than most, is a devoted, deeply-felt portrait of country he loved. He researched and compiled the text with an attorney's thoroughness and, indeed, it often reads like a brief, a compendium of information—gathered, filtered, processed, and presented to a jury of readers. If there is one caveat, it is that this is more a labor of love than a literary masterpiece. While not fraught with stiff legal vocabulary, neither is it a flowing book, enlivened with poetic prose. Cogently written, straight-forward, intelligent, and a *locus classicus* on the Great Basin, it is a priceless marker of time and space, a compendium of valuable observations, and an indispensable baseline. A reader responds to its accuracy of detail, not its lyrical syntax.

Desert Waters was originally written as six articles in a series on the Great Basin lakes for the quarterly, *Nevada Highways and Parks*, and expanded to treat the whole of the Great Basin and the rivers involved in the ancient lake systems. As Houghton himself wrote in the preface, the book was an "idiosyncracy: the choosing and assembling of various histories, organizing them with a particular point of view and setting them forth in a personal way" (14–15).

The original *Desert Waters* was published over a decade ago, and some of the minor annoyances as well as the visual snags carry over into the new edition. The original had a decent index, not as good as it might have been; one wishes it had been restructured. The black-and-white photographs of the hardback, slightly blurred at first because of printing on a non-glossy stock, have re-reproduced as well as might be expected. The paper of the reprint is slightly off-white, which may lessen definition still further. Neither the selected bibliography (twelve pages worth) nor the skeletal chronology have been updated. The precise maps remain indispensable.

In the new edition, Jesse Jennings has added an appreciative fore-word, and a section of well-chosen color photographs by Philip Hyde adds visual enjoyment although the format limits them in size and sweep. They catch the subtle monochromes and the vastness of the Great Basin and add considerably to the book's visual appeal.

The publishers state in their own preface that they decided not to edit or revise the original text, a determination with which I heartily concur. But so much has happened in the decade between the first edition and reprint, that I wished for an update of the chronology, or an "afterview" or "addendum," to say nothing of a list of more current works added to the bibliography. This is, after all, a reference book and these aids are what would make it more valuable.

Houghton poses many questions that have since been answered, and how they have been answered should be of interest to anyone who takes the time to read this book. The environment, both natural and political, has changed more than Houghton could have forecast. Not the least of these changes is the rise of the Great Salt Lake, the loss of migratory bird habitat and farmlands, and the political decision to pump excess water into the "West Desert." Smaller conundrums lie unanswered. For instance, Houghton described the island in Pyramid Lake with its fine population of pelicans, then endangered by lowering water which eventually would have made the island available from the mainland and thus allowed an influx of predators. Has this happened or not, and what of that population today?

Houghton ended with a chapter called "Energy Sources." It is outdated as far as information on solar energy goes, and dates the book. A note might have been in order: what has the progress of solar energy been since Houghton wrote? What do we know that he did not know? How has the energy situation changed? As the editors note, tampering with the text was not necessary, nor was a full-scale critical essay needed, but a simple annotated chronology of what has happened since 1976 would not only be helpful but would underscore the accuracy and vision of the original book.

Houghton "never knew a place he didn't like" and his affection for the Great Basin comes through in his fine book (14). Despite my carping, I recommend it as a valuable, indispensable reference for any reader interested in western history, anthropology, philosophy, geology, and ecology, or interested in learning about that huge interior-draining basin gathering into itself the waters of its rimming mountains.

Colorado Springs, Colorado   ANN ZWINGER

Cutthroat: Native Trout of the West. By Patrick C. Trotter. Boulder: Colorado Associated University Presses, 1987. 219 pp. $29.50 paper.

Fishes of the Great Basin. By William F. Sigler and John W. Sigler. Reno: University of Nevada Press, 1987. 425 pp. $32.50 cloth.

The main thrust of *Fishes of the Great Basin* is that fish are interesting for several reasons and among these is sport fishing. Unfortunately, with rare exceptions, fish are not directly observable and fishing may be one of the few ways that we may closely observe fish and appreciate them firsthand and close to their natural surroundings. In the Great Basin most streams are too shallow, turbulent, or muddy for direct observation of wild fish. The reservoirs are too murky and the lakes, though clear, are too cold. Neither snorkling nor scuba-diving are very pleasant or successful ways for the casual amateur observer to go fish watching in frigid Lake Tahoe or Bear Lake. Perhaps the best way to appreciate the greatest diversity of freshwater fishes is vicariously through reading about them in books like this one.

The book's geographical coverage includes almost all of Nevada, somewhat less than half of Utah, large areas of California and Oregon, and small corners of Idaho and Wyoming. The separation in miles and description between the Bear River and Mojave River headwaters is great. The two drainages have little in common except that water from neither flows into the ocean. Adjacent streams in the same sub-basins of the Great Basin are often as isolated from each other as they are from other basins because neither has sufficient water to reach the other before evaporating or sinking into the earth. The potential for development of new races and subspecies in such environments is great and is what makes hostile desert environments so interesting to ichthyologists.

A chapter on the history of sport fishing, subsistence fishing, and management of both kinds of fisheries records changing values. It also aids understanding the present distribution of native and introduced species. The number of citations suggests extensive research, although some old-timers will remember things differently; they always do. The philosophy, history, and content of the Endangered Species Act, though not the most interesting discussion in the book, is very relevant to fishes of desert regions. The Siglers list fifteen species containing at least one subspecies which is threatened or endangered among forty-four native species.

The chapter on evolution and classification of fishes is marred by ambiguous indication of the hierarchy of some major taxa. In a book aimed at the non-ichthyologist formal taxonomy should not be emphasized, but if the names of taxa between class and order (subclass and superorder) are listed, the authors should somehow indicate their relation to inclusive and subordinate taxa. The relationships among the living archaic ray-finned fishes (not spiny rayed fishes as printed) suffer from this omission. An indented outline or changing type font would have cleared up any confusion. Another alternative would have been to omit reference to major taxa not represented among recent Great Basin fishes. Additional confusion is created by the inference that gnathostomes (jawed vertebrates) are now extinct. If they are, we are all fossils. The brief discussion of more recent fossil fishes of the Great Basin is germane and clearly written, however.

An identification key to Great Basin fishes by Gerald R. Smith of the University of Michigan seems clear, simple, and useful. The drawings of separation characters are faithful to the species represented even in bare outline, in contrast to the crude sketches often used in keys. The key should be easy for amateurs to use in its limited reference to dissections and frequent reference to color and markings of live fish. I have not used the key, however, and that is the true acid test.

The chapters about the extant species of Great Basin fishes are, of course, the core of the book. The authors discuss each species under eleven topics of interest. These are: importance, range, description, size and longevity, limiting factors, food and feeding, breeding habits, habitat, and preservation. The narratives are in the unemotional prose of fishery management literature as the discussion headings suggest. They are, however, sprinkled with interesting asides and anecdotes. The compact, telegraphic style of the species narratives allows consideration of a diversity of topics in a moderate-sized book (10 x 7 x 1.5 inches), but it also leads to some problems. Seeming non-sequiturs, ambiguities, and contradictions occur occasionally. Most of these are due to an abrupt change of reference within a paragraph. Many would disappear with additional explanation and qualification.

Last to be considered but not the least of the book's attributes are the ink drawings and colored illustrations by Sophie Sheppard and Jim

Morgan. These range from fair to excellent. Drawings of the common carp, some of the chubs, golden shiner, Tahoe sucker, and a few others are standouts. These surpass the best photographs in conveying gross form and fine detail of the living fish. I also liked the colored illustrations apparently rendered from freshly caught specimens. The Lahontan cutthroat on the dust jacket is particularly appealing, though idealized in form.

Patrick Trotter is an amateur scholar of the literature about the cutthroat trout and an avid angler for the species. By "amateur," I do not infer ineptness but mean a passionate interest unusual in a professional scholar. He pulls diverse and seemingly unrelated topics together in narratives that demand close attention to keep track of the relation of disparate elements. History, Indian lore, anthropology, geology, fishing tales, landscape appreciation, and laboratory techniques are intermingled with accounts of the distribution, biology, behavior, and taxonomy of cutthroat trout in his book.

The native range of the cutthroat trout includes at least parts of all states and provinces west of the 104th meridian excluding Arizona and Texas. Vertically the species can be found from sea level to above timberline and Trotter seems to have personally explored most of these contrasting and far-flung habitats. He is not an armchair scholar. His introductory chapters define the cutthroat trout as a species and give general information regarding subspecies including present distribution, ancient distributions, and criteria and methods which ichthyologists use to recognize subspecies. Just when the reader might begin to feel well informed about cutthroat trout, Trotter reveals even more about each suspecies in separate chapters. It is not the kind of book one can enjoyably read in one or two evenings; to be fully absorbed, one would have to be a very erudite angler or a professional trout biologist. It makes a nice supplement to the professional literature on which it is based in that it adds angler interest and aesthetic appreciation.

Trotter's awareness of the tentative nature of current explanations of fish distribution and evolution and the subjectivity of subspecies is good. As he explains, we can only pass laws preserving a unique and isolated population of cutthroat trout after the population is formally described as a subspecies in the taxonomic literature. It is a melancholy thought that wild trout populations only receive protection when they are assigned a special status based on an untrammeled pedigree and when they are near extinction. Any self-sustaining population of wild trout, even if hybridized or not the correct subspecies, is a valuable thing at this late date and should be protected until it is replaced with the original subspecies.

Perhaps the most disappointing feature of this book is the poor reproduction quality of the photographs of trout and habitats. I suspect that most photographs printed were originally good color negatives or transparencies but suffered the loss of intermediate tones when reproduced in black and white. The color plates reproduced from paintings are interesting but seem to have been done from fantasy as much as from real specimens. They all appear a bit overly muscular and malevolent. I appreciate the attempt at subdued colors but they still are not quite realistic. Few artists have mastered trout colors.

A diffuse belief in the power of a science that produces lasting, ever-accumulating generalities to save threatened nature pervades both books and many other natural history books. We expect measurement and analysis of nature to reveal broadly applicable and precise regularities that will allow us to undertake actions or prohibitions to protect plants and animals and their habitats despite encroaching civilization. Practitioners of applied ecology maintain an unwarranted belief in the effectiveness of scientific method. The range of recent opinions among mainstream savants of scientific logic extends from the view that scientific method is a hopeful but fallible protocol to the view that it is complete nonsense. Whatever residual merit formal scientific method retains for theoretical physics, its logic denies it to the diffuse search for consistent associations in the unrestricted wild nature that characterizes applied ecology. The validity of ecological findings must be upheld by subjective agreement.

The common characteristic of all applied physical science, "exact" predictability, is absent among the phenomena lumped under ecology. What most practitioners of applied ecology fail to discern is that all science that yields exact predictions is limited in scope. Scientists will consider all failures to predict as the result of incorrect methodology or application to areas beyond the scope of the supporting theory. To say that ecological predictions are generally inexact is to say they are generally insufficient for practical purposes. We may physically isolate and protect ecological phenomena in a laboratory, but then they are removed from the infinite mutual relations which are ecology. Predictions may be greatly improved in the laboratory but the experimenter is then playing a different game. An ecosystem always has vague and shifting boundaries and scope.

Thus, studies on the relation of fish population numbers and biomass to various common habitat factors never explain even half of the practical variability occurring among these attributes in samples of lakes, ponds, and streams. The literature of fish ecology and management is composed almost entirely of accounts of studies which, for practical purposes, are inconclusive. Occasionally predictions based on these studies come about but so do those by anglers, bartenders at fishing resorts, loggers, and old game wardens. Science cannot take credit for successful predictions and recommendations that are the result of good luck or common knowledge. Any success in the protection of wild fish populations is usually due to intensive monitoring, specific experience, and subjective judgment. Canny fishery managers realize that fish populations fluctuate widely or disappear for many more reasons than natural history studies or computer models will ever include. Unpredictable and even unusual events that cause great changes in fish populations are common over periods as long as an ecologist's career.

Though descriptive natural history by itself is incapable of supporting precise predictions and recommendations, it does generate amateur concern and enthusiasm. By doing so it builds constituencies of nature advocates whose collective will may be at least as effective as scientific fact in preservation efforts. Beyond any practical function, the vicarious appreciation of nature through reading and television viewing is arguably as important as any other kind of entertainment. The direct observation of nature, as inspired by reading and television, is probably even more justified. Natural history need not masquerade as science to be vindicated nor does it need to render a proper deference to science. Its only requirements are that it be reasonably accurate, well written and entertaining. *Fishes of the Great Basin* and *Cutthroat: Native Trout of the West* are this and more.

Fort Collins, Colorado   WILLIAM J. McCONNELL

The Last Grizzly and Other Southwestern Bear Stories. Edited by David E. Brown and John A. Murray. Tucson: University of Arizona Press, 1988. 184 pp. $24.95 cloth.

Meet Mr. Grizzly: A Saga of the Passing of the Grizzly Bear. By Montague Stevens. Reprint. San Lorenzo, N.M.: High Lonesome Books, 1943, 1987. 281 pp. $12.95 paper.

Humans are fascinated with bears. Grizzly bears, in particularly have a certain mystique: they evoke feelings of fear, power, danger, and intimidation. Grizzlies can reach 800 pounds or more in size; the skin alone can sometimes be so heavy as to cause a pack animal to collapse under its weight. A grizzly can easily kill a cow, breaking the animal's neck with a single blow to the head. Although they generally avoid confrontations with people, these bears will attack if cornered or wounded. Even with a bullet through the heart, a grizzly can still charge and travel far enough to maul or at least thoroughly scare most humans. Yet we have always been curious of grizzly bears, even as they disappeared from the Southwest.

Two recent books display that curiosity, while putting the demise of the grizzly in a historical perspective with the expansion by humans in the Southwest. *Meet Mr. Grizzly,* first published in 1943 and now re-issued in a softbound version, is still highly readable. It recounts the exploits of a one-armed Englishman, Montague Stevens, who operated several ranches in New Mexico in the late 1800s and early 1900s. Stevens's knowledge of grizzly bears was gained from years of hunting, often following his group of hounds along hot or cold trails for hours or even days at a time. As a consequence, the information he presented on the life history and behavior of grizzlies comes within the context of a hunter and rancher. He understood grizzly behavior, tracking, and bear habitat.

His early chapters consist of a series of bear-hunting stories and a dose or two of biology. The middle chapters only peripherally discuss bears, but rather outline in considerable detail Stevens's perceptions of how dogs follow scents, and his methods for training hounds, horses, and mules. Once trained, his hounds were widely known for their abilities to track bears, sheep, cattle, and humans. His training methods—based on obedience with kindness—were not widely accepted, but they appeared to work.

There is no question that Montague Stevens had an inflated ego. It comes across plainly in print, and he took great relish in describing his accomplishments and examples where others were proven wrong. Some of his opinions on bear behavior are today discounted, but most stand the test of time. His dog stories are fascinating, often humorous, and sometimes bittersweet. His account of the rescue at gunpoint of a prized hound from a group of "hard cases" who he had tracked for over sixty miles only reinforces the feeling that Montague Stevens loved his dogs. Stevens hunted for sport as well as to kill bears that were taking cattle and sheep from ranchers. He enjoyed the pursuit immensely and considered himself fortunate to live in a period when grizzlies were plentiful. It was only following a tragedy with his beloved hounds that he gave up hunting. In the twentieth century, he actively worked toward preserving the disappearing grizzly—but by then it was too late.

The last grizzly in New Mexico was killed just a few decades after Montague Stevens's final hunt. This account, and twenty-one other stories, are included in *The Last Grizzly,* a hardbound volume edited by David Brown and John Murray. This compilation provides a fascinating historical picture of man's interaction with grizzlies in the Southwest, from the 1820s to their disappearance in the mid-twentieth century. The editors (who each provide excellent personal accounts as well) have included stories, lengthy letters, translations, and chapters from books that have been selected as being reliable. Introductory notes provide some background on the authors and their contributions (including Zane Grey, J. Frank Dobie, and Montague Stevens), and occasional annotations keep the authors honest.

Editors Brown and Murray have made commendable selections and grouped them to provide a historical perspective. The first part deals with accounts from 1826 to 1890, when bears were plentiful and bear hunting was productive and dangerous. Mountain man Dick Wootton summed up the attitude of this period in 1850: "The proper thing to do when you see a bear is to kill it." Bears were so plentiful that one killed any and all, including cubs. In general, bears were not wasted, but provided welcome skins and meat for the successful hunter. Many of these encounters are vividly described—bloodily for both man and beast—and are quite readable, particularly the stories by Wootton and William French (1885).

The second periodized subsection includes accounts from the late 1890s to 1924, when bear attacks were more common as people (and particularly hunters) intruded more into grizzly territories. The range of stories includes acts of viciousness by men and the realization that most attacks by bears were brought about, not by chance encounters, but by hunters pursuing and wounding animals.

The third historical period, 1913–1935, was a time when bears were killing livestock in greater numbers and were therefore considered fair game for ranchers and professional hunters. One such hunter, Ben Lilly, employed by the federal government for predator control, boasted (probably truthfully) that he had killed 200 to 300 bears in his life-time, as well as some 200 to 300 mountain lions in New Mexico alone. The bounties paid for such animals were not insignificant. Lilly received $200 per month for his services in 1916. Jack Tooker recounted his encounters in the 1920s with a pair of livestock-killing grizzlies, for which he was to be paid $1100. He succeeded, but suffered a severe mauling in the process.

The book's final section deals with the period after 1920. The few remaining grizzlies were extirpated from southwestern states and northern Mexico. Carlos Bailón and A. Starker Leopold each vividly described the final relict populations that disappeared in Mexico by the early 1960s. It was a period when some avid bear hunters from earlier years publicly mourned the passing of the Last Grizzly, recognizing that each of them had played a role in frontier history.

Who was responsible for the decline of the southwestern grizzlies? It is difficult in retrospect to point an accusing finger. Hunters certainly played a role though, in most cases, they were engaged in legal and perfectly acceptable activities for the times. Elliot Barker, whose account of the killing of the last grizzly in New Mexico appears in *The Last Grizzly,* long believed that grizzly once fed on elk. Once elk herds were extirpated from New Mexico, bears turned to the increasingly available livestock—putting them into direct conflict with people. It now seems apparent that conflicts between ranchers and bears, declining food and habitat, and a continuing popularity of bear hunting for sport accelerated the decline of grizzlies.

A single bear may range over an area of ten to one thousand square miles, feeding on plants, fish, and mammals. "To him, almost everything is food except granite," wrote John Muir. But, when this food and habitat started to decline, bears ranged farther afield, encountering sheep and cattle, and inciting the wrath and bounties of men. Bears were safe only in isolated pockets, such as the Sierra de Nido, apparently the last outpost of grizzlies in the Southwest, which Leopold described from a scientific perspective. In such reduced numbers, even an isolated poaching could reduce a small population below the reproductive level for maintenance. Carlos Bailón's account of bear hunting in northern Chihuahua alludes to the break up of large rancheros during the land reforms in the 1950s as bringing about the final demise of the grizzly. Contacts between men and bears were inevitable and, without protection, the bears disappeared.

Both *Meet Mr. Grizzly* and *The Last Grizzly* are well worth reading: one as an account of how things once were, and the other as a historical transition from that period to the present. Today, we hopefully know something more about land development and the management of unique wildlife like the grizzly bear. But, for the Southwest, livestock concerns now take precedence, and the time of the grizzlies has passed.

Zoology Department
University of Maine
Orono, Maine

John R. Moring

High Noon in Lincoln: Violence on the Western Frontier. By Robert M. Utley. Albuquerque: University of New Mexico Press, 1987. 265 pp. $22.50 cloth.

Merchants, Guns and Money: The Story of Lincoln County and Its Wars. By John P. Wilson. Santa Fe: Museum of New Mexico Press, 1988. 226 pp. $24.95 cloth.

It is a shame that these two volumes, both of which focus on the Lincoln County War in New Mexico (although they are hardly identical in approach or coverage) appeared at exactly the same time. One of them is likely to be lost in the shuffle, and it is unlikely that it will be Robert Utley's follow-up to his recent *Four Fighters of Lincoln County* (Albuquerque: University of New Mexico Press, 1986). Utley's name on a book has become a hallmark of high quality, and this latest volume from the retired National Park Service historian is right up to his usual standard. But Wilson, a Museum of New Mexico historical archaeologist who is an expert on Lincoln County, has written a good book, too. Like its rival, it is even-handed and fair, taking no sides in the "war." It is well-written and thoroughly researched. As is its competition, the volume is equipped with historical photographs and more than adequate notes, bibliography, and index.

Wilson's book actually differs a great deal from Utley's. Where the latter focuses very tightly on the events of the so-called war of the late 1870s, Wilson covers the entire history of the town and county, from the former's founding as *La Placita del Río Bonito* to the shift of the county seat from Lincoln to Carrizoso in 1913. The most interesting section is that treating the violent years, but the background information on the area and its earlier conflicts, such as the Anglo-vs.-Hispano Horrell War, the Tularosa Ditch (i.e., water) War, and the Pecos (range) War explain the county's continuing climate of violence. The post-1880s material is of less value; then Lincoln was just another sleepy western town in decline.

Wilson's is a good book, but Utley's is the better of the two. If a collector, student, or library could only buy one of the two, it would have to be his. But, ideally, both should be secured and shelved together, for their viewpoints and contents complement each other. Utley's research is up to that of Wilson and, as usual, his interpretations and insights are excellent. He is much the better writer. The "ranger" has mastered the very rare skill of dramatic narration which takes no liberties with historical fact. His books, including this one, *do* "read like novels." Only one minor complaint can be lodged, perhaps, against Utley. He does intrude into the narrative on rare occasions to inform the reader, omnipotently, what *should* have happened. Thus, Sheriff "Dad" Peppin and Jimmy Dolan "should" have stood trial, for example. Such meddling with the historical record is a historiographical kapu that probably should not be violated.

Since Utley's powerful research lens is poised over the Lincoln County War, per se, and particularly the climactic five-day battle in the town itself, his is the more consistently interesting text. In both books, however, all kinds of fascinating details are woven into the story. Some are important: Mrs. McSween assumes a more important role, and Billy the Kid a much lesser one, than writers of popular history have suggested they should. Others simply supply human interest: one of the men who tried to fire McSween's house was a deaf-and-dumb fellow known solely—and cruelly—as "Dummy." Or, one of the cowboys, Gus Gildea, a veteran of the California Lava Beds campaign against Captain Jack, gave a new name to the Regulators, once they were on the run; he called them "Modocs."

Both books set the record straight; the Lincoln County conflict was a war without heroes, unless we count minor characters or major figures on the fringes of the action. (Perhaps cattleman John Chisum and the Army's Captain Carroll qualify.) The "good guys" of the romanticizers, greedy partners McSween and Tunstall, end up looking no better than the members of the entrenched Murphy-Dolan-Riley ring. Colonel Dudley's possible good intentions were weakened by his drinking and his superior's orders, so he wobbled back and forth. Small wonder Governor Lew Wallace would try to make him the scapegoat of the affair. Even Sheriff Brady and posse leader Dick Brewer, seemingly decent men, were tarnished by the climate of violence and had their characters besmirched by selfishness, rabid partisanship, or adherence to the lethal code brought to New Mexico by typical Texan hardcases. The Lincoln County War was simply a dirty little fight for money and power—mercantile monopoly—in a backwater county whose only sources of wealth were the contracts to feed the army at Fort Stanton and the Indians on the Mescalero Reservation. Nobody came up smelling like the proverbial rose after this bloody and unnecessary affair.

While Wilson's volume is, seemingly, the more general study, it is actually upstaged in this regard by a final chapter in Utley's book, "Post-Mortem." This summing-up explains the generalizing subtitle, "Violence on the Western Frontier." The author makes a case for the Lincoln County War being a model of frontier psychology during the

Gilded Age. In New Mexico, rugged individuals, mostly young, rootless bachelors, whose "crutches" were booze and firearms, performed the same, sad, drama that was played out, with only slight changes of script, in Tombstone, Arizona, or Johnson County, Wyoming. Where courts were feeble and peace officers no better than the outlaws they faced (and the army under orders not to intervene in civil matters), nature, abhorring a vacuum, allowed violence to fill the place of law and order.

Librarian Emeritus   RICHARD DILLON
Sutro Library
San Francisco, California

Two Guadalupes: Hispanic Legends and Tales from Northern New Mexico. Edited by Marta Weigle. Santa Fe: Ancient City Press, 1987. 164 pp. $7.95 paper.

Few researchers, apparently, have taken advantage of the New Deal phenomenon called the Federal Writers Project. Very likely the project has been regarded as simply the "make work" kind of recovery activity that it was supposed to be. As a consequence, the products of that project have generally gathered dust in somebody's archive.

Luckily, Marta Weigle, New Mexico folklorist, has taken advantage of this resource by utilizing the folktale collections of Lorin W. Brown and Bright Lynn. The two Guadalupes were two women who told Brown and Lynn beliefs and old tales—of magic, of legendry, and even the type called "fairy tales" for want of a clearer title. Weigle put the collection into perspective by adding biographies of the two ladies who told the stories for decades to the children of their neighborhoods, plus vintage photographs of their lives and church activities, around which some of the stories revolve. The result is a rich resource indeed, made even more valuable since one of the tellers is a city dweller, and the other from a small village.

One tale of interest involves variations of the European story of John the Bear (Aarne-Thompson Tale Type 301), source of the Anglo-Saxon classic *Beowulf.* In New Mexico the union of bear and girl that produces the prodigious child is left out, the account focusing upon Juan Oso's rescue of the stolen princesses, his battles with monsters, and his presenting proof that he, not a usurper, deserves the prize, the hand of the youngest princess, of course! (Presumably he got the rest of the girl, as in hundreds of European fairy tales, although in one Texas variant, "Catorce" [Fourteen], the hero was interested only in consuming fourteen of everything—cows, barrels of drink, etc.)

The reader learns about the time Saint Peter lost the keys to Heaven and was saved from disgrace by an angel in disguise, and the old familiar story of the boy Saint Christopher carrying Christ across a river—with a human touch added, when the boy complains about how heavy Christ is. There are tales about enchanted princesses, a donkey that supplies whatever its owner needs, a prince transformed into a bird—quite a full range of folk tales is delightfully present here.

Other familiar tale types appear in rudimentary form, because of the nature of folk transmission. Beginnings are omitted, conclusions or morals left out, and events swapped around—but the flavor of the folk tale is generally rich and full in its presence. Witness "The Three Treasures" (Tale Type 707), a story reminiscent of Haroun Al Raschid: the king has the habit of going out among his subjects in disguise, hoping to get the word straight from the folk. On one such journey, he overhears three daughters confessing their dreams: one wants to marry the king's cook, so she'll have plenty to eat; another loves pastries, so she wants to marry the king's baker; the third wants to marry the king and have beautiful golden-haired children. The king arranges that each gets her wish, but the two sisters who aimed low are envious, and gang up on the third. While the king is off in battle, the wife gives birth to a baby girl; the sisters have the child stolen and send the king word that she has given birth to a puppy! They repeat the ploy twice more, except that the second and third children are boys. Assuming that his wife has played him false, the king has her buried up to the neck, so that passersby can spit on her. A gardener raises the three children, with wigs covering their golden hair. Ultimately, after a series of adventures by the boys, plus marvels galore, the king gets straightened out, takes his poor wife out of her living grave, and—to the surprise of no one—they all live happily ever after, except for the wicked sisters, who are punished!

Weigle has done a fine job of providing critical apparatus—appendices, sources, notes, and even a map—to make this collection far more than just a group of charming tales. The similarities of remote New Mexico to the Old World come out in the presentation, showing clearly that folklore lives on, especially among close-knit cultures like New Mexican Hispanics. The non-folklorist will enjoy the stories in their variety and color, while the specialist in folklore, anthropology, literature, and a variety of other disciplines will find ample food for study here. The enduring qualities of the folktale are present, but the richest reward is in the revelation of the inner qualities of the culture of the Hispanic Southwest.

English Department   JOHN O. WEST
The University of Texas at El Paso